FORGOTTEN
HOSTAGES

A Personal Account of
Washington's First
Major Terror Attack

PAUL GREEN

FOREWORD

This book is about the first major terrorist and hostage incident in Washington, DC. If you were to look up terrorist activities on the Internet for 1977, Wikipedia has one page listing 13 events around the world. If you queried 2008, there are 41 pages of events; 2009 has 33 pages, and 2010 had 104 pages.

One of the 13 events listed in 1977 was the terrorist siege where I and numerous colleagues were held hostage and two other buildings were attacked. In March 1977, Washington, DC, was brought to a standstill for almost 40 hours with a coordinated attack on three separate locations: the District Building, the seat of government for the District of Columbia; the Islamic Center, which housed a mosque on Massachusetts Avenue along what is known as Embassy Row since many countries have their embassies in this area; and the B'nai B'rith building on Rhode Island Avenue. B'nai B'rith at that time was a 147-year-old organization dedicated to helping bring Jewish people together to promote and represent Jewish causes. It was also an avenue for community service work, providing services and activities for Jewish teens and college age students.

This terrorist siege became an international media event widely covered by television and print media. It also happened at a time when there was neither commercial Internet nor cell phones. How information was being disseminated and shared as the event unfolded provides an interesting look at a different world than we know today with our instant communication and sharing of events both large and small through cell phone, Blackberry and a host of other technological wonders.

There were numerous components to this terrorist event: the hostages and their families; colleagues of the hostages; the terrorists who perpetrated their hatred and venom; the story of how the terrorist siege came to be; the police, FBI and other government agencies that were engaged during the

40 hours of terror; local and national political leaders; international diplomats; and representatives of the media who at times became active players in the event.

In the District Building, a little known council member almost died from being in the wrong place at the wrong time. Some years later, Marion Barry would become Mayor of Washington, DC.

For a young reporter named Maurice Williams, also at the District Building, his fate was not to be as positive as the council member.

As time has passed, and as I researched further what I had seen, experienced and knew, a number of ironies or coincidences came to light. Some I can't fully explain. I'll describe some of these circumstances and let readers reach their own conclusions on how situations and facts intersect.

During and after the events of March 9 -11, 1977, I vividly recall the sights, sounds and smells that were associated with what we lived.

A number of years ago, I turned the event into a management program relating it to various aspects of management and leadership to senior executives in the financial services sector. The reaction has been fairly universal. It is a compelling story and still incredibly relevant today to what's going on in the world.

The next inevitable question is "When are you going to write the book? Why haven't you done so in all these years?"

There are numerous reasons. Would anyone really be interested in the story? I've been busy with my career over the years and could I make the commitment necessary to do what would be required to get it into my lap top? One nagging question I've always had is where do I start?

I was one of the younger executives in the organization at the time of the siege—27. As I've gotten older, moving beyond "middle age" the realization that time is not infinite becomes more of a stark reality. I remember when our family friend Allan Mann hit 50 which was14 years ago. I joked with him that I couldn't believe I had a friend and golfing buddy who was that old.

Although I didn't keep in direct contact with many former colleagues, Washington is like a small town in America where you can keep track of people. I realized a number of my former colleagues had passed away and knew many were reaching a stage in their lives where perhaps their memories were less clear and they were concentrating on the inevitable health issues one faces as we grow older.

The prodding of colleagues and people who had heard the story and the situation that I described became the impetus for me to finally focus on what needed to be accomplished. I hope colleagues or others who were impacted by what occurred in March 1977, and read the words that I have written, will think that I have had represented their voices, thoughts and lives accurately.

In my mind, it is still a compelling story and highly relevant to what the world faces today. It is a look at the essence of terror and its impact on the innocent people who, through fate and happenstance, must endure the cruelty human beings can heap on fellow humans. It also depicts the human spirit that calls upon resources people do not know exist within them in trying to get through a very difficult time in their lives and to do so with dignity and their sense of humor still intact.

PRELUDE TO TERROR

One of my early offices at B'nai B'rith was adjacent to the Klutznick Museum. Philip Klutznick, a world renown businessman, philanthropist, future Secretary of Commerce and former President of B'nai B'rith, sponsored and funded the museum and also many other B'nai B'rith activities.

Everyday I'd view the letter the museum displayed from George Washington which he wrote in 1790 to the Toro Synagogue community in Rhode Island. He stated that the new country would not tolerate religious bigotry. Each day I looked at it as if I was doing so for the first time.

Soon after reading the letter on the morning of March 9, 1977, unbeknownst to me, seven terrorists had driven up to the front of the B'nai B'rith building and parked a U-haul truck literally at the front of the door. They actually brought the truck up on the walkway leading to the front of the building and placed it at the glass front doors.

The seven then proceeded to unload and carry with them 20 different firearms which included rifles and pistols, almost 9000 rounds of ammunition, three hatchets, 12 folding blade knives and straight razors, 10 fixed blade knives, eight machetes and seven other purses that contained ammunition. They had a number of what could be described as exotic weapons such as garrotes, strangulation instruments of Spanish origin, and a pungi stick, as well as some food for themselves.

187 years after Washington wrote,—"May the children of the Stock of Abraham who dwell in this land, continue to merit and enjoy the good will of other inhabitants. While everyone shall sit in the safety under his own vine and fig tree, and there shall be none to make him afraid".—my colleagues and I were about to face terror, religious bigotry, violence and threats of death.

CHAPTER ONE

THE BEGINNING

My first assignment for B'nai B'rith was as a New Lodge Director in Philadelphia–basically a community organizer trying to form lodges which were the core of the membership structure of the organization.

In the short time I was in the Philadelphia area, I read the *Philadelphia Inquirer* every day, having it delivered to our apartment in Lindenwold, New Jersey. Growing up in Miami, my parents instilled in me the importance of keeping up with the world, and reading the newspaper daily was a required ritual. I remember reading an article in the *Philadelphia Inquirer* about a hit squad of Black Muslims who had traveled from Philadelphia to kill someone in the Washington, DC area. They committed a horrendous crime, had been caught and were tried. Little did I know that a few years later, I'd be part of that story that had its birth a short time prior to us relocating to Washington.

After a few months in Philadelphia, I realized that being a new lodge organizer was not a long-term employment goal. I was extremely fortunate when Steven Morrison, the National Director of The Leadership Cabinet, pulled me aside at a conference I was attending at the L'Enfant Plaza Hotel in Washington, DC in July of 1974 and discussed a job as the Assistant National Director of the B'nai B'rith Leadership and Young Leadership Cabinet. Pretty heady stuff for a 24 year old. By September, the job was mine and in December, my wife Jane, eight months pregnant with our first daughter Emily, and I were relocating to the Washington area.

Over the next 18 months, I became part of the B'nai B'rith staff culture traveling the country and to Israel soon after the Yom Kippur War. It was great developing relationships and friendships with wonderful colleagues. I was also fortunate to be exposed to thousands of individuals who made up the volunteer leadership structure and gave their time, efforts and money to support B'nai B'rith's work across a wide spectrum. Two examples during my time with the Leadership Cabinet were Abe Kaplan, the Chairman, a successful businessman from Birmingham, Alabama, and Tommy P. Baer, a young attorney from Richmond, Virginia, who headed up the Young Leadership segment of the overall cabinet.

Historically it takes a long time for a young man to move through the chairs to gain the Presidency of B'nai B'rith. Tommy's climb was no exception. His commitment and tenacity took him to the top as International President from 1994 – 1998. He worked hard for many years and deserved it.

Towards the end of 1976, B'nai B'rith International was going through changes that had been brought on by a management change at the top executive level. At the September Biannual Convention that was held at the Washington Hilton Hotel, Dr. Dan Thursz was named the new Executive Vice President replacing Rabbi Benjamin Kahn whom I had known as Chief Executive since joining the B'nai B'rith staff in February 1974. Rabbi Kahn, the Executive Vice President from my start at B'nai B'rith was a nice man, but not a strong leader. When the Board of Governors made the leadership change they turned to Thursz who was the Dean of the School of Social Work at the University of Maryland. He also had a long history with the organization through his work with the B'nai B'rith Youth Organization, which I was intimately familiar with having been a BBYO leader growing up in Miami, Florida.

I didn't really know Dan that well, but knew of his reputation as a tough boss, a strong intellect and a style that took no prisoners. Dan was also physically intimidating—he was at least six foot seven.

To say that apprehension was rampant within the ranks of the B'nai B'rith staff while the convention was going on is an understatement. I had some brief conversations with Dan at the meeting that involved the normal exchanges of looking forward to working with one another. I know one of us wasn't being totally honest in that exchange.

The 1976 B'nai B'rith convention also became an indelible experience in my mind. It allowed me to work on a major event with thousands of people in attendance and also began the wonderful journey I have had in personally meeting numerous leaders of our country. The convention was just a few months before the 1976 election and since B'nai B'rith represented a large contingent of the Jewish community we attracted President Gerald Ford and his challenger Jimmy Carter, then Governor of Georgia. We also had an international evening with some 30-40 embassies represented by either their Ambassadors or a top embassy staffer. Carter gave his speech on one afternoon of the convention. He actually had a personal connection to B'nai B'rith. The person who became his White House Counsel was Robert Lipchitz an active member of a B'nai B'rith Lodge in Atlanta, Georgia.

President Ford followed the next morning. It was a short drive from the White House, and we were waiting for President Ford in a room with a private elevator from the street level. When the door opened, the number of people on the elevator was astounding—aides, personal assistants to the President, speech writers and a host of others.

Having a chance to meet these leaders at 26 years of age was truly exciting. It also allowed me to observe a number of things that were just fascinating about life, politics and the power of Washington. I've always had heightened observation skills and I was able to put them to good use. Little did I know that these observation skills would be tested to a level that I had never known in just six short months.

We also received a surprise—Henry Kissinger decided to address the convention to answer a number of Carter's assertions during his speech. When Kissinger arrived, I was standing with David Blumberg, the President of B'nai B'rith, off stage and right next to the Secretary. He truly did seem larger than life.

The whole experience of the convention in 1976 showed me that B'nai B'rith, in spite of challenges facing the organization, still retained a measure of respect and clout within the power scene of Washington, and had attracted people from the highest levels of government to participate both nationally and internationally. I thought it was an impressive show and the members felt the same way. I didn't know at that time but B'nai B'rith's perceived statute both on the national and world stages was also being viewed by someone with a much more nefarious idea in mind than what people at the convention were feeling. The people at the convention were part of a vibrant institution that represented the high ideals of democracy and community service.

CHAPTER TWO

LEADING UP TO THE SIEGE

Following the convention and true to form, Dan's style was tough. He obviously had ideas on how B'nai B'rith should be functioning and what kind of changes were needed to try and help revitalize an organization that had lost membership and fund raising dollars. One of his favorite ploys when he saw you in the elevator or in the hall way was to quickly ask what exactly were you working on. You'd then try to explain on one foot how important your work was to the organization and why you were needed. It didn't take long to realize that it was just as convenient to visit colleagues on different floors via the stairwell. A few months in the future the stairwells at the B'nai B'rith building would be ingrained in my mind for the remainder of my life.

At the same time the management changes occurred, the leadership of the organization in 1976 made a decision to construct a mirror image wing to the existing building. The building that I went to work in in December 1974 on Rhode Island Avenue was eight stories high with two elevators and two stairwells. The building housed both B'nai B'rith International and B'nai B'rith Women, which operated as separate organizations. The original structure could not house all the staff who worked for both organizations. My first office was on the 2nd floor and was probably a cleaning closet at one point. After that, they relegated me to the 8th floor, which was turned into a cubicle city where B'nai B'rith and B'nai B'rith Women staff were co-mingled.

When they finally started to de-construct the 8ᵗʰ floor and start over in that area, I was relegated to another part of the building. Then they put up a few nice cubicles in the library on the ground floor and that's where my office was located. Jeff Rosenfeld, a young attorney who was serving as the Legacy Director at the time occupied the cubicle next to mine. It was just the two of us. We had developed a friendship and also commuted together. He'd drive in from Columbia, Maryland, and we'd head in from our apartment in the White Oak section of Silver Spring, Maryland. I actually enjoyed the atmosphere where our offices were located. It was quiet and the cubicles were made of rich wood. It was the nicest work area that I had at B'nai B'rith.

It was also adjacent to the Klutznick Museum. Philip Klutznick, a world renown businessman, philanthropist, future Secretary of Commerce and former President of B'nai B'rith, sponsored and funded the museum and also many other B'nai B'rith activities.

Everyday I'd view the letter the museum displayed from George Washington to the Toro Synagogue community in Rhode Island where he stated the new country would not tolerate religious bigotry. Each day I looked at it as if I was doing so for the first time.

I also developed a wonderful friendship with Anna Cohn who had become the museum curator at a young age. Anna was smart and insightful on a wide range of issues and I always looked forward to our discussions. Her career since B'nai B'rith has been quite expansive with stints at the Holocaust Museum and handling an important program for the Smithsonian for many years.

The construction of the new wing commenced and as we watched the building evolve we developed a tolerance to the associated noise and inconveniences. During late 1976, the library area was exposed to the outside and some plastic sheeting was hung. I remember coming in one winter morning and finding my assistant Harlene Dodis sitting at her desk with her overcoat on, wearing her gloves and trying to type. It felt like it was 40 degrees where my office was situated. I sent her home to enjoy the warmth of her apartment.

Harlene's father was the President of one of B'nai B'rith's largest Lodges in the Northern New Jersey area. She worked for me for a short time and I was sorry when she left. But, alas, marrying the dentist of her dreams was more important than typing the endless internal memos B'nai B'rith was famous for during those times.

As with any organization, there was speculation as to where you'd end up and what your work surroundings might look like once the new wing was completed.

It's important to reflect on the security considerations that existed at the B'nai B'rith building. Basically, there were none. Perhaps a harbinger of what could be a problem should have been more carefully examined and studied. On March 5, 1975, I was out of the office for the day and when I tried to call through the switch board a young voice that I had never heard before answered the phone. Twelve young men and women from the Committee Against Israeli Retreat, which had been born from the Jewish Defense League, had rushed the building and taken over the switchboard of B'nai B'rith and also occupied a few staff offices.

The group wanted B'nai B'rith and other Jewish organizations to denounce and work against what they called the "Ford-Kissinger policy of strangulation of Israel." They used a megaphone to shout out their feelings through open windows. The police were called and after awhile the protestors left the building and no one was arrested. For many of us, it was almost a humorous occurrence that a bunch of college students had taken over part of the building and disrupted the organization's operations.

One colleague, George Spectre, who was involved in our international programs and who always expressed strong feelings about such activities, took this action as a fore warning of things to come that would prove to be more accurate. He had a premonition that something worse would occur.

George's work on international matters exposed him to more situations and people who worked on issues that could be harmful to the Jewish people. He had developed a much darker perception about any incident where people could take over and disrupt a building, particularly a building that represented Jewish interests. The rest of us obviously were more naïve about such matters. When an incident would occur, George would make his thoughts known to B'nai B'rith management in his usual forceful manner. His opinions on security matters did not gain much traction for I didn't notice any increase in security at the building.

The building wing was almost completed, and I finally had my first permanent office on the 5th floor in the new wing. Work continued on other floors and a part of the new 8th floor area was still under construction. A good piece of the floor was a shell. The details of the building and various aspects of my colleague's lives would become an intimate part of my life and thoughts. These thoughts and details are still a clear vision even after 34 years. None of us who worked at B'nai B'rith during this time thought we would become part of a terrorist act that would receive international attention. To this day, people pulled into the unfolding situation often reflect on how it impacted their lives in some manner.

CHAPTER THREE

MARCH 9, 1977 – TERRORISM ARRIVES IN WASHINGTON, DC

My morning on March 9, 1977 started with coffee in Fae Hoffman's office, the Executive Director of B'nai B'rith Women. I met Fae when I first joined B'nai B'rith in 1974 and she was working in the career and counseling area. We had a chance to get to know one another at the District 3 Convention in June of 1974 which was held at one of the resorts in the Catskill Mountains in upstate New York. District 3 represented B'nai B'rith Lodges in the New Jersey, Pennsylvania and Delaware areas. In the mid-70's Fae had become Executive Director of B'nai B'rith Women while she was in her early 30's—quite an unusual feat.

That morning, we were discussing a potential singles' retreat that would require cooperation between B'nai B'rith Men and B'nai B'rith Women. At that particular time of both organizations' history, there was some level of mistrust about motives. Because the women felt the men wanted to fold them into their organization, a simple program such as a singles retreat for men and women from both organizations was a radical idea.

In 1971, B'nai B'rith International created Units which allowed for men and women to belong to the men's organization. Over coffee, we were trying to decide whether to go ahead with plans or cancel the program due to various problems that were cropping up. We were heading to the same conclusion that it wasn't worth the aggravation and it would be best to cancel.

After a brief discussion with Steve Morrison about my talk with Fae, I was typing at Linda Radin's desk. She had been my assistant for a short time and had just left the organization.

I was working on a memo that Dan Thursz had requested from all the executives. In my mind it was just another intimidating gesture on his part that he asked us to provide an explanation of what we would like to do in the organization if our present job did not exist. We knew that Dan was here to change things. Whether the request had true meaning was questionable though the rumors of reorganization started to make the rounds among staff members.

At 11:00 that morning, there were loud noises coming from the floors below. I looked at Harriet Berman, the assistant to Steven Morrison and me, and we both had quizzical looks on our faces. The noise was becoming more pronounced and I also heard the sound of glass breaking; it kept getting louder. I told Harriet I would go down and take a look. I walked down to the second floor stairwell and standing about 10 feet from me were two black males. They were throwing objects left in the stairwell by the construction crew down to the first floor landing. One of them told the other to pick up a piece of metal or piece of glass or a ladder and throw the item down the stairs.

I did not see any weapons, and they did not notice me standing there watching them. I looked up and saw two colleagues looking down at me; one was Norman Buckner and the other was Billy Clamp from accounting.

As we continued to watch the men throw items down the stairwell, a few other colleagues joined Norman and Billy. They asked me what was going on. I figured they were two construction crew workers who had been fired from their jobs and were taking retribution against the building. There didn't seem to be any other explanation to what was happening.

After watching for a few minutes, still unnoticed by the two men, I went up to the third floor and walked with Norman, Billy and others to the third floor elevators situated in the original part of the building.

Shortly, Stephanie Snyder from the accounting department came out from her area just around the corner from the elevator bank, in front of Jerry Rudman's office. He was B'nai B'rith's controller. She said she heard there was a gunman in the lobby of the building. I also saw Ralph Basellero from accounting standing in a storage closet next to the elevators looking confused and scared. He had his hand on the door knob and his actions indicated that he would like to just close that door and get on with his morning.

There was another noise coming from the stairwell in front of me and I walked over to look down. The next thing I saw were three gunmen running up the stairwell. The first one was coming up the stairs two to three at a time and he had two pistols.

I did not grow up around guns and had fired a gun just a few times in junior high school with Gil Johnston, a boyhood friend growing up in Miami. We'd visit his sister and brother-in-law in an undeveloped section of southwest Miami where we could set up targets and shoot.

Though my experience with guns was limited, I had read enough about weapons to realize this gunman was waving a .45 Colt pistol and a .357 magnum. They were big, powerful and ominous weapons.

As compared to seeing the two men on the 2nd floor level, this time I was seen and he was yelling at me to freeze where I stood. The warning was laced with obscenities and threats. I backed away from the door and the first gunman, who was waving two pistols, came through the door. He had a big smile on his face and said that if we didn't hit the floor and stay down, we would all be killed.

I didn't realize at the time that I was just introduced to the second in command, Abdul Latif, aka Carl Roper. He was 34 years old and already had a criminal record dating back a few years. It certainly was a one-way introduction.

Prior to hitting the ground, I noticed the other two gunmen were carrying carbine rifles. Already they were starting to yell obscenities and instructing people to follow their directions or they would be killed. I dropped to the ground where I was standing and my first thoughts were that this was a robbery. I was prepared to offer my wallet and whatever else they wanted.

Commotion seemed to be building with each passing moment. I heard a lot of shouting, screaming and things breaking. I also thought I heard a gunshot for the first time. I wasn't sure how many of us were lying next to the elevator but knew it was a sizable number based on the group that had been trying to figure out what was happening in the initial moments.

Unbeknownst to me at this time was that seven terrorists had driven up to the front of the B'nai B'rith building and parked a U-haul truck literally at the front of the door. They actually brought the truck up on the walkway leading to the front of the building and placed it at the glass front doors. I guess they didn't realize that B'nai B'rith did not offer valet parking. In fact, the few parking spaces the organization had in the basement level were sought after commodities. They were held by long term employees and were viewed like Washington Redskin season tickets. You just hoped you lived long enough to earn one of the coveted spots.

The seven then proceeded to unload and carry with them 20 different firearms which included rifles and pistols, almost 9000 rounds of ammunition, 3 hatchets, 12 folding blade knives and straight razors, 10 fixed blade knives, 8 machetes and seven other purses that contained ammunition. There were a number of what could be described as exotic weapons such as garrotes, strangulation instruments of Spanish origin, and a pungi stick as well as some food for themselves.

They entered the building and moved to take control of the elevators to cut them off at the ground floor. A young colleague, Steve Widdes, who had taken over the Legacy Director responsibilities from Jeff Rosenfeld, appeared and was pistol whipped. With his head bleeding, he was put on the floor and instructed not to move.

Anna Cohn, the Director of the Klutznick Museum, heard the nearby commotion and quickly realized the need to find a safe hiding place. She climbed up towards the ceiling, pushed out some ceiling tiles and hid there.

Once the ground floor was secured the terrorists brought the elevators to the second floor and started to move through the building from the stairwells. The terrorists were very familiar with the building. A number of them had served as construction workers while the building was being built. A few of them posed as delivery men or just meandered into the building to scope it out– further indication of how secure the building was.

They knew of the two elevators, two stairwells as well as obstacles that might need to be overcome. Lying on the third floor I still thought it was a robbery and didn't realize that many of my colleagues were facing decisions that would impact their lives.

CHAPTER FOUR

LAWRIE'S STORY

One such decision was being made by my colleague and friend Lawrence Kaplan, more affectionately known as Lawrie. He was the Director of B'nai B'rith's extensive insurance program and his expertise helped deliver about $4 million to B'nai B'rith at that time -a nice tidy sum. I'm not sure if they truly appreciated Lawrie's efforts. I first met him in February 1974 when I joined B'nai B'rith and Lawrie was working in the membership area that I had just joined. He quickly became a friend and mentor and took me along on a trip to Chicago soon after I joined the staff so I could gain some real life experience. I got a chance to meet Lawrie's son Jonathan, who was five years old at the time and was going to visit his grandparents. I had mistakenly dropped a piece of paper while waiting for our luggage and I was appropriately chided by a five year old for creating litter.

As the incident within B'nai B'rith began to unfold, Lawrie was visiting with Albert Elkes, B'nai B'rith's membership director in his office on the 5th floor. Al and Lawrie were close friends and Al originally brought Lawrie to B'nai B'rith in the membership area. While in Al's office, Lawrie received a call from his assistant Becky to let him know that a gunman was just seen walking around the 3rd floor where Lawrie's office was situated.

Lawrie had served in the Army and was trying to figure out what was happening. His training taught him not to run into something he didn't understand until he got a clearer picture. He told Becky to go into his office and try to take as many people as she could with her, push up his desk and other office furniture against the door and then get on the floor and remain as quiet as possible.

At the same time, Albert's secretary came in quite anxious about the news that was starting to circulate around the building and she bolted from his office to try and escape. Where to exactly she most likely had not figured out. Albert decided to take off after his secretary before Lawrie could stop him. His actions would prove to be a miscalculation. Albert Elkes was probably one of the gentlest human beings one could want to know and I'm sure his concern for people was inherent in the action he took in going after his secretary. He didn't know what he was walking into.

After I joined the staff in February 1974 and was visiting B'nai B'rith for a meeting, Albert had me out to his apartment in Arlington, Virginia, to meet his partner Eddie and enjoy the view of Washington, DC, that Al and Eddie enjoyed every day. When Emily was born, Al presented Jane and me a beautiful silver spoon. He said Emily should be born with a silver spoon in her mouth. It was classic Al.

As the noise was becoming more pronounced, Lawrie quickly determined that he needed to gather people who were milling around into Albert's office for safety. By the time he closed the door there were 12 people crowded into the office.

Lawrie was beginning to hear a loud commotion building as well as gun shots. He pushed Albert's desk and other office furniture against the door and told everyone to lie on the floor and be quiet. He had no idea what was going on but felt his actions were starting to be based on a survival instinct.

It was just after 11:00 am, and the first major terrorist incident in the United States was gathering steam. Lawrie's actions were a determining factor that 12 of my colleagues were not to be fully exposed to what was going to play out at the B'nai B'rith building. After he barricaded the door to Al's office, Lawrie and the group of colleagues were stuck on the 5th floor for a good part of Wednesday, March 9th. As Lawrie looked out the window he saw police arriving, a huge amount of commotion on the streets surrounding the building and activity from adjacent buildings.

Later in the afternoon, reporters had gained access to offices in buildings across from Lawrie's line of sight and they were holding up signs asking who he was. He returned the favor and held up a sign asking who they were. Lawrie didn't know that his picture was also being taken and it would appear in publications around the world.

CHAPTER FIVE

MY JOURNEY TO THE 2ND FLOOR

Back on the 3rd floor, I was lying in front of the elevator bank, still not sure how many of my colleagues were with me, but convinced a number of us were concentrated in that small area.

The noises coming from various parts of the building grew more pronounced. The terrorist continued to scream at us not to move and to do so would bring death. In these initial moments I still thought we were involved in a robbery. What else could it be? Lying on the floor, the noise, shouting and commotion were increasing. I thought I heard more gun shots that sounded like loud firecrackers.

After a period of time we were told to stand up. They were going to march us, one at a time, down the stairwell to the second floor. Abdul Latif was standing a few feet off to my left screaming instructions. He had the two pistols, one in each hand and was yelling obscenities at us. He threatened to kill anyone who made sudden movements.

I noticed another terrorist had stationed himself at the door leading to the stairwell. He had a semi-automatic gun trained on us. This was my introduction to a third terrorist, Abdul Adam aka George Smith, 31 years old. As we stood, I noticed that Norman Buckner, was first in line. I had seen him above me when I was in the stairwell on the 2nd floor landing watching the two men throwing construction items down the stairwell. The terrorist gunman in the stairwell pointed his gun and motioned for Norman to move. Norman disappeared around the door into the stairwell.

I was then a bit mesmerized as I looked at the man standing in line in front of me. I had no idea who he was. He was tall, skinny with blond hair and wearing glasses. I thought I knew the vast majority of people who worked in the building even though there were nearly 200 employees at 1640 Rhode Island Avenue. I was processing this information, but for the life of me, couldn't place who this individual was.

It wasn't until later that I found out how this gentleman came to be in the building that day. His name was Jay Nichols. He worked for IBM and came in that morning to service typewriters. He probably thought his day was going to be like any other– go to work on his calls, do his job and go home to his family– just like all of us did that day.

I can't imagine what was going through his mind at that very moment. Did he want to say, "Pardon me, but I really don't belong in this building and if you don't mind, I'll just excuse myself and head out of here and get on with my day". I think that's what I would be thinking if I was in his situation.

As the day progressed, I began to realize there were numerous people in the building who were unrecognizable to B'nai B'rith staffers. By fate and chance they found themselves in the wrong place at the wrong time.

As Jay Nichols walked to the door, the gunman in the door well hit him square in the face with the butt of the rifle. It sounded like a big thud. It broke and knocked his glasses off and he fell to the floor on his back.

His face was bleeding and I could see that he was in pain and in shock. He had done absolutely nothing to provoke such a violent action. Abdul Adam was screaming at him to get up but he didn't seem to be able. I bent down to help him and Abdul Adam stepped out from the door well and poked me with the gun on the shoulder to backup. This went on for about 30 seconds and Adam was becoming agitated that Nichols could not get up. They finally dragged him to his feet and pushed him down the stairwell.

At this point I was trying to further process what was happening. My first inclination, that we were involved in a robbery, was quickly beginning to subside. Though events were unfolding at a fast pace, I also seemed to be viewing images in slow motion and in what I could only describe as a heightened Technicolor. It was as though I was looking at a movie seeing vivid details and the bright colors that were associated with the surroundings. Unfortunately, my colleagues and I were part of the cast of characters whether or not we wanted to participate. The intensity of taking in the sights and sounds were increasing exponentially at a rapid rate. It was almost like being an observer on the side watching the events unfold. My various senses seemed to push into overdrive. I didn't realize it at the time, but my body had already started to change both physiologically and psychologically.

Abdul Adam then motioned me to move and as I walked by him, he told me he would kill me. He took his carbine rifle, swung it at me and hit me on the side of my face with the metal barrel. I quickly looked back at him, he yelled an obscenity at me and he once again threatened to kill me if I didn't get down the stairs. My immediate thought was that I couldn't believe he hit me and that he just broke my jaw. It certainly felt like my jaw was broken.

I didn't know it at the time but the zygomatic bone on the right side of my face was crushed and my upper cheekbone was broken in six different places from the bridge of my nose to my ear. Just like Jay Nichols, who did nothing to receive the punishment meted out by the gunmen, I now had been physically assaulted.

Abdul Adam was showing me that he could do whatever he wanted and the demonstration was duly noted. I continued to walk down the stairs, I put my hand to my face, took it away and saw large amounts of blood were dripping from my face onto my shirt and pants. I was now in the stairwell all alone, bleeding quite heavily with blood soaking my shirt.

Every day I had walked the stairwells between floors instead of taking the elevators. It was quicker and provided some exercise. I never gave it much thought. Now, the stairwells of the B'nai B'rith building would have a measure of reflection for the rest of my life.

At that very moment, for some reason that I can't fully explain, I thought to myself I'd just walk out of the building. I had decided that was my mission. In the very short time between getting hit in the face and starting to walk down the stairs I truly believed that I would accomplish just that. It occurred to me the point from where I was standing to walking out of the building was not very far. I should have realized that such thoughts were either foolish or delirious. I just didn't know the extent of what I was going to be involved with. If I had known what lay ahead, my thoughts would have been more sober. I now had my head down and was picking up speed and was concentrating on doing what I decided.

Unfortunately my mission came to an abrupt halt. I literally ran into a man standing on the 2nd floor landing of the stairwell and we hit chest to chest. We bounced off one another and the sound of doing so was quite profound even with all the noise that was cascading around us. The blow of hitting each other forced me back up a few steps and he was knocked backwards a few steps. I don't know who was more startled.

I didn't know at the time that I just encountered the leader of the terrorist group, Hamas Abdul Khaalis, aka Ernest Timothy "XX" McGhee. He was a man of medium height, had a goatee and, even for his age of 56, seemed to be built fairly solid. Unfortunately, I had intimate knowledge of that fact. He was standing there with a pistol. A few other gunmen were standing near him, each armed with a handgun or a rifle and also had long knives and a few had ammunition belts around their chests.

After I bounced off his chest, all of them started to laugh. I guess they thought it was a humorous moment. I wasn't sure what was going to happen next and at that point my highly tuned sense of humor was not very active. Khaalis, the man who was blocking the way down to the lower floors, pointed his pistol at me and directed me towards the doorway on the second floor landing. This led to the area that housed the offices of B'nai B'rith's fund raising operation. It looked like my plan to just walk out of the building was not going to come to fruition.

The 2nd floor reception area, 20 feet by 20 feet, had never been utilized. The two elevators were in this area. As I passed the other gunmen, they said to run in through the door and jump into the pile.

The scene on the 2nd floor was beyond description. There were bloodstains on the immediate wall to my left, to the wall in front of me and the wall near the fund-raising office doorway. In that small area I encountered a pile of people– men and women piled on top of each other. I had just stepped into a world that was filled with confusion, fear and a struggle to comprehend what was happening. I stepped through a few people and fell towards the pile, not landing completely on my stomach, but on my side. My intent was to try and not injure anyone as I fell into the group.

Other colleagues continued to enter the 2nd floor area. Based on the events that took place over the previous 15 minutes, witnessing the violence against Jay Nichols, having my upper cheekbone busted and seeing other colleagues being injured, one could quickly surmise that the pile of people I just joined on the 2nd floor was being created for execution. It was about 11:15 am and people thought they were going to die. But this was just one area of activity in the earliest moments of the siege.

CHAPTER SIX

MARILYN'S STORY

On the 7th floor, Marilyn Bargteil, a wonderful lady who had a clear headed view of life and a sense of humor to match mine, was also trying to figure out what was going on in the building. Nancy Steel, Dan Thurz's secretary, approached Marilyn's desk to say she had received a call that there was a gunman in the building. Marilyn could see that Nancy was extremely upset. Marilyn had worked at B'nai B'rith for a number of years and had been through a few of the small incidents in the building when people just fluffed them off as non-occurrences and thought more of the same was happening. She walked Nancy back to her desk and tried to reassure her that everything would be ok.

At that time, Alton Kirkland, one of the young black men on staff, had gone from the 7th floor to the 5th to see what was happening. He encountered some of the gunmen as he looked from the stairwell. They told him to freeze but he ran back up to the 7th floor. When he saw Marilyn and a few others he told them what he had seen and said they should find a place to hide. She thought that was good advice and told herself that's what she was going to do and tried to convince others to do the same.

Finally, 13 people crowded into Yale Goldberg's office. (he was the Director of Administration and was not in the office that day). As they went into Yale's office they also closed and locked the door to Shirley Figenbaum's office, Yale's assistant. Shirley's area was in an enclave just outside Yale's. As Marilyn looked around the room, she saw Hank Siegal, from the PR Department; Bernard Simon the PR Director and also head of the B'nai B'rith Pension Fund; Shirley Feigenbaum, Lil Schevitz who was Ben Kahn's former assistant and now handling items for Dan Thursz; Nancy Steele; Hannah Sinnauer who handled the Office of the volunteer President of B'nai B'rith; Joe Sklover, B'nai B'rith Chief Financial Officer; his assistant Evelyn Ellis; three other colleagues Sandy Rosen, Sara Bloom and Maxine Rosenthal; and Alton Kirkland.

Originally Si Cohen, head of B'nai B'rith's community volunteer efforts, was near the door but he decided that he didn't want to be locked in a room so he left and his assistant, Dorothy Glazer, followed him.

Marilyn was confused by what was happening. She looked out the window and saw that police were around the building. They didn't seem interested in the section of the building she was in but were looking at the new wing. Shirley Feigenbaum called 911 and asked that police help be sent. Marilyn was still working off what she heard, there was a lone gunman in the building, and was not feeling scared. They received a number of calls in Yale's office from colleagues who were in other offices, frightened and asking for help.

One call came from Fae Hoffman, Executive Director of B'nai B'rith Women who I had coffee with early that morning. Fae asked if they could call the police and ask them to send help. Marilyn suggested that people stop looking out the window since no one knew who might be looking in. Perhaps someone could shoot at them through the window.

After another 911 call they decided not to use the phone any longer becoming more alarmed that someone might see the light on other phones somewhere.

Marilyn thought whoever was in the building was looking for the leadership and once they knew they were not there, would leave. Certainly nothing wrong with wishful thinking, but that was not the case. They finally heard sounds in the hall. Someone was shouting obscenities and wanted them to open up the door. When they didn't respond, it was kicked in.

She didn't realize at the time that she had just encountered the second in command, Abdul Latif, who was joined by Abdul Adam, the man who had hit me in the face with the rifle. The terrorists obviously had a plan to take over the building floor-by-floor through the stairwells.

As Latif came in he said, "Look what we have found, there's the rabbit", as he pointed at Alton. Latif admonished him for not listening when he was told to stop when they saw him in the stairwell on the 5th floor and for not opening the door when asked to do so. They had Alton spread eagle on the floor and frisked him. Then they finally brought everyone out of the office into the hall way.

Latif left and when Adam saw the closed door across from Yale Goldberg's office he told Alton to kick it in. With some effort he did and as he backed away, Adam became enraged and drew a long knife. He stabbed Alton in the leg and again in his side. Alton cursed him and Adam said he was going to stab him in his heart. He tried but instead stabbed him one more time in the side and Alton collapsed on the floor.

Marilyn was beside Alton when the attack occurred and was pushed back into a wall hitting her head. She didn't realize at the time that she had ruptured a blood vessel and would soon have trouble with her vision. The people who witnessed the attack on Alton were horrified and thought he was dying as they watched. Sandy Rosen, who had some first aid training, asked if she could try to stop his bleeding. Her initial request was refused and she was told to stay where she was. By this time, Latif had returned and was upset at what Adam had done while he was gone and told him to get back to his post.

The pleading to help Alton continued and at one point, Latif put his gun to one woman's head and told her she was dead if she didn't remain quiet. He finally acquiesced and allowed Sandy to administer first aid. Her selfless actions, in spite of the threat to her own safety, probably saved Alton's life.

The group that was captured on the 7th floor was now instructed to walk single file toward the stairwell where they were going to be taken below. Latif indicated that Alton needed to be taken as well. So a number of people helped carry him to the stairwell. He continued to bleed as Sandy tried to administer aid.

As they got to the stairwell, they saw colleagues from the 8th floor, under gunpoint, making their way down the stairwell. At one point, there was enough congestion in the stairwell that people had to wait for others to get by. Marilyn recalled it was like they were at a stop sign waiting for traffic to clear.

They finally reached the 5th floor. As Marilyn came out the stairwell door, she saw a pile of 50 people in front of the elevator bank. They were told to pile on top of people already lying on the floor. Marilyn, who kids about her weight, was made to lie on top of Dick Burg from the Israel Commission area. Her first thought was poor Dick; she was going to crush him and whispered apologies to him. Alton was placed off to the side and Sandy continued to administer to him as she asked people for handkerchiefs and other items to try and stem the bleeding.

As Marilyn and others were struggling to comprehend what was happening to them, colleagues in other parts of the building were also becoming absorbed and entangled in the terrorist siege. They just didn't know or understand the magnitude of what was occurring and would be happening to us.

CHAPTER SEVEN

THE BEGINNING OF BJ'S ORDEAL

Betty Jean Neal was on the 6th floor when she encountered the terrorists. BJ, as she was universally known in the organization, had come to B'nai B'rith in March of 1973 after losing her job at another company.

She had noticed a help wanted ad B'nai B'rith had placed in the Sunday paper. She had limited knowledge of Judaism and though that wasn't a prerequisite, she thought it would be useful to work at a Jewish institution in the relationship she was building with a former neighbor who had become a constant companion and happened to be Jewish.

She started in the adult Jewish education area, worked for a short time in accounting and was now the secretary to the Director of Personnel, Dale Bell. In the early morning of March 9th, BJ had a physical and got to the office at about 11:00 am. If that physical had been delayed a short time, BJ probably would not have been played a key role in the first major terrorist siege in the United States.

BJ had just taken her coat off and hung it on the door of the small temporary office that Dale was using before his new area was ready. She was approached by Gail Fruhling, a young employee of B'nai B'rith Women who told her she heard there was a gunman in the building. BJ thought, as many of us on the staff did that once again, some crazy college students were looking to interrupt our day.

Now she was hearing loud noises and commotion from throughout the building. BJ ushered Gail back into the small office and they decided to just remain there and be as quiet as possible. Then they heard a noise just outside the door. BJ's comment to Gail was whatever was happening in the building, had arrived at their door.

She put Gail behind the door as it was pushed open and saw a man with a gun and various knives hanging from around his neck who told her to come with him. BJ wasn't sure why, but she asked the gunman whether she should bring her coat? She didn't know that she wasn't going to need her coat for some time.

As BJ left the office the door was closed. The terrorist did not know that Gail was behind the door and she was left in the office. BJ was led to the elevator bank area and saw colleagues already lying on top of one another and was told to pile on.

The terrorists asked everyone if they knew if there were others on the 6th floor that were hiding and if they did, they had better tell them or all of them would be killed. No one said a word.

After a short time, BJ was instructed by one of the terrorist to get up and come with him to check other offices on the 6th floor. She was told to open each door and then he would search. One of the last checked was the office where BJ was captured. The door was half frosted glass and Dale and BJ's coats were still hanging up obscuring the office. That was a lucky circumstance since Gail, who had been told to stand behind the door, was obviously where BJ left her since BJ had not seen her.

BJ thought to herself,—"Gail, if you even move or make a noise, I'll kill you myself." BJ slowly opened the door and the terrorist looked in. With Gail standing behind the door, hidden by the coats, saw no one. He was satisfied that no one was hiding in any of the offices they had searched.

He took BJ back to the front of the elevators and had her lie down on top of people. Sometime later they were taken down to the 5th floor to join their colleagues lying on top of one another in front of the elevators. For Betty Jean Neal, the next 40 hours of her life would be something she would remember forever.

The group lying on top of one another on the 5th floor were finally asked if there was a large area or conference room where everyone could be taken. Responding that the 8th floor was under construction, they were told to stand up and go up the stairwell to the 8th floor. They were one of the first groups to be taken there. That group, which now included Marilyn Bargteil and BJ Neal, made their way, conga line style, back up three flights to the final destination where all of the members of the B'nai B'rith staff who were captured would be spending the next 40 hours.

They were marched to the back of the room and told to lie face down on the hard cement floor. Next, they were instructed to stretch out and hold onto the feet of the person in front of them–all of this with a constant stream of obscenities and threats of death. The gunmen began a count of the number of people captured. Obviously math was not their strongest suit and it took them several attempts to get the correct number. Marilyn and BJ remember vividly the number they confirmed at that time—100. They didn't realize more would be added. Their point of reference, as was mine, was strictly taking in what was happening in front of us.

The terrorists also had colleagues carry Alton up the stairs to the 8th floor and Sandy continued to work to save his life asking the terrorists for something to stem the bleeding. At one point Abdul Adam told her he "saw the hate in her eyes and that she was just a Jewish whore and when they started their work, she would be sorry."

Sometime later, after much pleading that Alton was going to die without medical attention, they placed him in one of the elevators and sent him down to the bottom floor. Although seriously wounded, Alton crawled out of the elevator. At first the police did not go near him, fearing that he might have be booby trapped with explosives. Alton finally convinced them he was a B'nai B'rith employee and was rushed to the hospital.

CHAPTER EIGHT

THE 2ND FLOOR LANDING. THREATS OF DEATH AND THE ANTI-SEMITIC TIRADE BEGINS

Back on the 2nd floor, people had to walk across the pile to get to an area where they could fall down. As people came in after me, the pile was so deep that their feet did not touch the ground. I felt a few others run across me and across others.

Mimi Feldman from Hillel fell on top on my left hand side. She was in her 50's and was crying and saying, "oh my God no, oh my God no." I turned my face back to look at her and she became hysterical. I was bleeding heavily and it was harder to see out of my right eye. I was able to grab Mimi's hand and tried to calm her down telling her everything was going to be ok. I'm sure she didn't believe me.

Mimi seemed to calm down a bit and we were looking at each other–I tried to smile at her. It was almost as if we were the only two people in the room and were concentrating on one another. Even with the horrendous situation we were beginning to experience, Mimi, like a typical Jewish Grandmother which she was, said that she wished she had a handkerchief or a tissue to give me to try to stop the bleeding. Since I could not get my face down on to the carpeting, the bleeding continued.

With violence and the threat of death swirling around us, Mimi Feldman reached out to me with compassion and caring. She did so in spite of the tremendous fear I knew she was feeling at that very moment. I have always had a very positive view of life and that feeling has never subsided. My wife Jane and daughters Emily and Jessica kid me that this view is so far from reality and that I live in my own little place and the rest of the world just isn't like that.

At that particular moment of my life, at 27 years of age, a very conscious thought occurred to me and I said to myself quite clearly that I was bleeding to death. Whether the facts were physiologically accurate or not, I repeated to myself in my mind several times that I was bleeding to death. For a period of time I felt this to be a fact. I knew that I needed to try and stem the bleeding or I was in trouble. At that juncture my rosy outlook on life was being severely challenged.

From that thought I moved to one where I would try to get to the bottom of the pile and have a chance to try and press my face against the floor. I also felt that lower in the pile was safer than being near the top as the situation continued to become more severe and threatening. There was no question that self preservation thoughts entered my mind as well.

I looked across to my left and saw Jerry Rudman, Controller of the organization, lying with his legs out in front of him and his back against the wall. Jerry looked like he had a bullet wound just above his eyebrow—there was a distinct hole evident there. His face was bleeding heavily and blood was dripping down to his shirt. One of the terrorists had confronted Jerry by his office and hit him with either a pistol or rifle butt. Jerry was caught just above his eyebrow and we must have looked like we were seeing a reflection of ourselves in a mirror.

As I looked at him, he caught my glance and we nodded. We communicated with our eyes the disbelief of what we were experiencing. All we could do was shake our heads no and this certainly summed up that we had no idea what was happening to us.

I started to work my way into the bottom of the pile and looked back towards the front of room and noticed Wesley Hymes lying perpendicular to me. Wes, B'nai B'rith's printer, looked as though he was in a great deal of pain. I asked him if he was ok and he informed me that he had been shot. I believed that the pool of blood coming from Wes was from his shoulder wound. Later I learned that the wound responsible for the majority of blood was from a machete slash across his hand which he held near his stomach.

Wes was working at his printing press that morning on the 2nd floor near the mailroom and storage area and did not hear the commotion occurring near him. As he worked, he was tapped on the shoulder; when he turned around, one of the terrorists wanted to know if he was deaf and why he wasn't following their instructions. Wes was a solidly built young black man.

That combination became dangerously serious for many of the young black men that worked on the B'nai B'rith staff. They became instant targets of the terrorists, who were quickly enraged about the fact they could be working for white people, particularly those who were Jewish. Young men, whether white or black, seemed to be natural victims of violence. There was no question in my mind the terrorists felt that if anyone was going to try and put up any fight, it would be young men and they did not hesitate to neutralize that threat. In reality, there was a mismatch from the beginning. It was going to be tough to fight carbine rifles, shotguns, .357 magnums, .45 pistols and machetes with Cross Pens. To this day, I wonder if they would have brazenly come into the building if they thought everyone inside had similar weapons to protect themselves.

The terrorist who confronted Wes swung his machete at him. Wes tried to deflect it, but suffered a deep cut across his hand and then ran towards the 2nd floor landing. It was at this point that Wes was shot with one of the .357 Magnum pistols. The force of the blast lifted him off his feet. He said it felt like he did a full twist and a gainer before hitting the ground. The terrorist who shot him came over, cocked the pistol to shoot him again when Khaalis came around the corner and told his comrade to leave him where he was. Wes became the bottom of the pile on the 2nd floor.

I also noticed a pool of blood on the leg of someone lying just in front of me. He was wearing jeans and a checkered shirt and I didn't recognize him at first. It was one of the carpenters who must have been working in the building that day, he was lying down in the pile of people, his feet in my face, and I thought he had been shot in the leg. That wasn't the case because one of the terrorists yelled at him to stand and throw his tool belt out into the open area. He stood up without any problem, threw his tool belt, and got back down again.

Then I realized that the blood on his feet was coming from Wes who continued to bleed heavily. I noticed Lew Hamburger, the Assistant

National Director of the B'nai B'rith Youth Organization, off to my left near Jerry Rudman. Lew was on his knees. He turned his face towards me and mouthed the words, "Are you shot?" I indicated no and he just shook his head at me, then turned to Jerry and asked him the same question. Lew got no reply since Jerry's glasses had been knocked off and he was probably close to legally blind without them.

A short time later, Sam Fishman, one of the Rabbi's from the Hillel staff, was thrown into the room, landing in the far corner on the right side with his back up against a wall. Sam's glasses had been knocked off and he was holding a handkerchief to his eye, which was bleeding quite profusely. At first it appeared that Sam's eye had been taken out. As I looked at him, I was having trouble comprehending how a gentle Rabbi, a Rabbi who worked with college students to help them define their lives, had been beaten and perhaps just lost his eye.

Terrorism knows no bounds. It doesn't discriminate among its victims. It absorbs and consumes all that are in its path.

I looked around the room and did not see my colleague Steven Morrison or Fae Hoffman or others whom I had seen earlier that morning. I figured that perhaps they were on the bottom of the pile. Everything was in such disarray and people were keeping their heads down. I looked across the room and saw a man who looked like Max Baer. Max had been the National Director of the B'nai B'rith Youth Organization for multiple decades and had turned the reigns over to Sid Clearfield. It would not be unusual for Max to visit and I thought he had picked a less than desirable day to do so.

I later learned the man was Gerd Strauss. Gerd was a volunteer member of B'nai B'rith who lived in the Washington area and bore a resemblance to Max. He obviously had made a bad choice that morning coming in for a visit. Gerd was a dedicated volunteer who cared about the organization and he was now part of an event whose final determination was far from being decided. I never knew why Gerd happened to be in the building on the morning of March 9th.

As for Sid Clearfield, he was captured as well and was in the pile of people on the 2nd floor. At one point in the siege, Khaalis threatened to cut off Sid's testicles, stuff them in his mouth, cut off his head and throw it out the window to show the authorities that he meant business. If Khaalis wanted to carry out this threat he could have done so. We were powerless to respond to this act of terrorism.

We didn't know it at the time, but essentially we were going to live our lives minute-to-minute. Based on what our eyes were seeing and our ears were hearing, our brains could only process that what Khaalis and his men were threatening was real.

As I looked at Sid, I figured he truly could use one of the countless cigarettes that he smoked during the day.

His intake of cigarettes was impressive and when I would visit him in his office, he had this huge round ash tray and it was filled with more butts that I could count. I always wondered what his wife Lois thought of his smoking habits. He had his doctorate in social work, had served as the Dean of the School of Social Work at a major university and was a bright guy. He was a nice man as well and I'm sure he was wondering as were all of us, was this truly our last day on earth.

The chaos on the 2nd floor was real. People were frightened, confused and many thought their last moments on earth were confronting them. It was becoming difficult to breathe in the pile as more people were added from the floors above. I thought that everyone captured by the terrorists at that time was in this small confined space. It wasn't until later that afternoon that I realized the terrorists had consolidated the building in a few areas. People captured from the 4th floor down were being hoarded with me on the 2nd floor and those captured from the 8th floor on down to the 5th had been piled in front of the elevators on the 5th floor.

The B'nai B'rith building, on the morning of March 9, 1977, had been turned into a war zone. It was intense and violent, and my colleagues and I were about to experience things that would remain with us the rest of our lives.

Observing what was transpiring around me, another thought came to mind. It was about the book that I had read the previous summer concerning the Munich massacre of the Israeli athletes. I recalled the event clearly. After I graduated from the University of Miami and before I started my first full time job in September of 1972 at the YM-YWHA of Northern New Jersey, I had a summer job loading trucks and picking up trash at a new store called Builders Emporium in Wayne, New Jersey.

I was recovering from knee surgery and Jane and I were living with my in-laws prior to moving into our own apartment. My father-in-law Sidney thought that even though I was recovering from surgery, I was more than able to work for the summer. He would leave the employment section on the table for me to read each morning while I had my coffee. Never one to be subtle, I think he mentioned to Jane every day that he couldn't understand why an able bodied young man couldn't be working. I thought my knee surgery gave me a pass, but I finally took the hints to heart and I started to work in late June. My trash pick-up mates called me professor since I had a college degree and I was the only one who would read *The New York Times* during our 15 minute coffee break off the food truck in the morning.

By the end of July, as I assimilated with my new colleagues, the most important thing I thought about was what Jane had packed me for lunch. The store had a great TV section and during the Olympics I would do a quick walk through the area to catch a glimpse of the events, particularly the swimming with Mark Spitz.

When the terrorists struck the Jewish athletes in the Olympic Village I made more frequent stops to see what was happening in Munich. The book I read the summer of 1976 described in vivid detail the violent take-over of the apartment complex where the Israeli athletes were staying. Islamic extremists were involved in the brazen attack. I could not comprehend the notion that I was reliving that scene that was so easy to imagine from the descriptive writing in the book. It also occurred to me that the athletes did not survive their terrorist siege. Those who had survived the initial assault had been killed during a failed rescue attempt at the Munich airport. The terrorists turned on them with guns and hand grenades as they realized they were being attacked by German security forces. The details and chapters of the book literally flew through my mind as if I was speed reading.

I thought of Janie and Emily, but not in the context that I would never see them again. I was wondering and said to myself, who would come to stay with them during the ordeal. I was thinking this situation would last a few days and we would come out of this ok. I can't explain why I had such thoughts or why I had come to that conclusion. Perhaps it was a defense mechanism that kicked in and allowed me to have some hope that we would survive what we were experiencing.

At that particular stage, lying in a pile among colleagues, being threatened with death, it certainly was not one of my most rational or logical thoughts. Based on our situation, it would have been more realistic to think that our lives were in imminent danger and might be shortened beyond what ever natural determinations exist for a person in the world. But that was not how I was starting to think.

Jane and I had met during undergraduate school at the University of Miami. We sat next to each other in Professor Milstead's criminology class, and she did a lot better than I did and is certainly a lot smarter than I would ever be. When we were first married, she taught at a private school in Miami and didn't particularly like it. After Emily was born, she wasn't sure what she wanted to do. Thinking she might be interested in physical therapy, she was taking a few classes at the University of Maryland since she didn't have a lot of science courses in her background.

Jane had dropped Emily off at day care on March 9th. Sponsored by Montgomery College, we were eligible to use it since she was at school all-day taking classes. She had no idea how my day was going and didn't find out until much later in the afternoon that I wasn't coming home from the office that day.

When she arrived at the day care center, one of the teachers came out to meet her and was visibly upset and seemed to be crying. Jane immediately became concerned that something had happened to Emily. The teacher then said she was sorry about her husband—meaning me– and Jane had no idea what she was talking about. When Jane asked her what she meant the teacher explained that the B'nai B'rith building had been attacked that morning. The teacher informed her that she had another girl at day care, Jennifer Rudman whose father worked for B'nai B'rith. It was Jerry Rudman's youngest daughter and his wife Paula was trying to arrange to get her. At that time, Jane did not know the Rudman's but agreed to take Jenny home once she learned that Paula and Jerry lived just a few minutes from our apartment in Silver Spring. This happenstance allowed the development of a friendship between Paula and Jane that would last many years and a close bonding of the Green and Rudman families. Jane and Paula had no idea what Jerry and I were enduring and that we both had been injured in the initial moments of the siege.

I continued to believe that somehow we were going to come out of this ordeal which would allow me to deal with the violent events that were happening around me. I was willing myself to believe that I was not going to be killed on this day and that I would see my family again and experience a life that I thought I was going to enjoy.

The other conscious thought I had at that moment was to say to myself that I wanted to concentrate on everything that was happening to me and my colleagues. To take in our surroundings, to absorb everything–sights, sounds, smells and conversations. I wanted to create a picture in my mind that I would never forget–to recall everything. I was determined not to miss anything.

Ever since I was a kid, I had a special talent to remember literally everything. I'm not sure you'd label it a photographic memory, but I could visualize things in my mind that allowed me to store incredible amounts of information about people, places and situations. I remember specific details from more than 50 years ago as if they happened yesterday. I'll remind someone of something that happened a lifetime ago and get a blank stare in response from them. And now, that God given skill set was to be employed to capture this event.

I started to fully concentrate on the immediate events that were happening around us. I noticed that Brian, a young man who was working with us in membership, was lying next to me. He had bumps all over his face, was bleeding from the nose, and it looked as if he had been beaten badly. He looked like he was in pain, scared and confused as the rest of us. I asked him quietly if he was okay and he nodded. We looked at each other for a short time with our eyes trying to comprehend what was occurring.

At this juncture, the pile of hostages was probably three to four feet high and people had stopped being added to the pile. Being on that 2nd floor landing was terribly frightening and very explosive in the sense of not knowing what would happen next. If you were to take a vote at that time and said let's have a show of hands on how many people think they are going to die, I would have bet the vast majority of people would have raised their hands. The intensity of the moment was severe.

That people were being piled on top of one another was incredibly disconcerting. If one could be totally rational during the situation, you could have logically reached a conclusion that the group of people in the pile was being readied for execution. What other conclusion could there be? That colleagues had suffered violent attacks further added to the heightened awareness of the difficult situation. The space where we were piled was very confining and cramped. I was situated towards the center of the pile and could make out what was happening in front of me and to my left. It was difficult to try and make out what was happening behind me. Though the circumstances were very difficult, ironically, lying with colleagues in the pile had a mild calming effect. I could see that people were able to hold hands together, to give nods or whisper some form of encouragement or just ask someone if they were ok. We gave strength to one another by communicating with our eyes and a feeling of being close.

We then met the leader of the terrorists for the first time. It was the man I ran into on the landing and had bounced off of chest-to-chest. He began an anti-Semitic tirade laced with obscenities and informed us that the Jews had created all the ills in the world. He said that we didn't deserve to live and that the world would be a better place if we didn't exist.

When I was growing up in Miami, occasionally I would experience some type of action that could be labeled anti-Semitic. In most instances, these occurrences were done by non-Jewish friends who were making a comment out of ignorance and parroting something they heard from their parents or other friends. I also recalled a presentation by a member of the John Birch Society to our AZA Chapter in Miami, (the Jewish youth group affiliated with B'nai B'rith). He was a friend of our adult advisor. His presentation was laced with innuendos about Jews. I recall those in the group who were older than me became visibly upset at his comments and a physical confrontation almost occurred that evening.

What my colleagues and I started to experience on the 2nd floor landing was so far beyond anything I had ever experienced before. It was startling for its ferociousness and raw anger. The vindictiveness of the delivery suggested that Khaalis did not develop these feelings and perceptions overnight, but that a lifetime of hate was spewing out at a rapid pace. As he screamed at us that we didn't deserve to live, he did so with a strong conviction and I knew that he meant his words.

He began to talk about the horrible murder of his family in 1973. Why we didn't support him in his time of need? When he asked a question of the group, demanding that we answer yes to him, he wanted us to reply yes sir.

37

He said that now we would have to show him respect for he was in charge of our lives. For many of us, this was the first time in our lives we had no control over an outcome that might determine if we survived the next few minutes let alone the remainder of the day. We were helpless. Khaalis and his men could have done anything they wanted and we did not have the capacity to influence the direction of the unfolding events. One had to wonder if God had the capacity to answer all the calls being made at that particular moment.

CHAPTER NINE

HAMAS ABDUL KHAALIS

Hamas Abdul Kaahalis had been one of the top leaders of the Black Muslim movement. After Malcolm X, a Black Muslim leader, became disenchanted with Elijah Mohammed, the movement's leader, Khaalis concurred with his feelings and became a follower of Malcolm X.

Khaalis's thinking and feelings became further radicalized after Malcolm X was murdered. At that time, Khaalis formed an orthodox sect that had more defined fundamentalist beliefs, the Hanafi movement in Washington.

The movement's headquarters was set up in a nice home in the northwest section of Washington on 16th Street right next to a synagogue. Directly across the street was another synagogue. The home had been purchased for Khaalis by the NBA's great basketball star Kareem Abdul-Jabbar who had become a follower of Khaalis. As his spiritual leader and mentor, Khaalis had given the former Lew Alcindor his Islamic name. It is a name known around the world—a name that is synonymous with one of the greatest basketball players to have ever played the game.

Previously, Khaalis had sent a letter to members of the Black Muslim nation denouncing Elijah Mohammed as a false prophet as well as denouncing other members of the organization's leadership. This letter created huge anger at Khaalis. In January 1973, a hit squad of eight men from a Philadelphia area mosque associated with the Nation of Islam and known as part of the Black Mafia from that area, headed to Washington to kill Khaalis.

When Ronald Harvey, John Clark, James Price, John Griffin, Theodore Moody, William Christian and Jerome Sinclair arrived at Khaalis' home on 16th Street, he was not there. The killers entered the house and encountered his 23 year old daughter Amina, his 22 year old son Dawud, a younger son Rachamon as well as his youngest daughter Bibi and her three small children. The killers brutally murdered members of his family by shooting the adults execution style and drowning the kids in the bathtub. The youngest victim was Khaalis's nine-day-old grandson. It was truly a horrendous act and seems incomprehensible to anyone who has a thread of moral fiber in their being. One of his daughters had survived the attack after being shot numerous times and most likely would be in a wheel chair for the remainder of her life.

After the murder of his family, Khaalis felt the police were not truly engaged or interested in finding the killers. However, they were captured and tried in Washington. The judge who drew the trial was Leonard Barman who, coincidentally, was Jewish. During the trial, Khaalis questioned the judge's handling of the case and was emotional at times. His outbursts caused the judge to find him in contempt of court and he was ordered to pay $750. He was upset about this and considered the contempt citation as a further indication that the authorities were not concentrating on administering the necessary justice for the crime that was committed against his family.

Kareem Abdul-Jabbar was not the only person he mentored or gave an Islamic name. He mentored David Belfield who was born in North Carolina and raised in New York. Belfield came to Washington to attend Howard University. He was active in various black causes and also developed an interest in Marxist dogma. While in Washington he met a man who was a musician and Korean War deserter– Ernest "XX' McGee–who had become Hamas Abdul Khaalis. The same man who was now standing on the 2nd floor landing in front of a pile of people.

Khaalis counseled his protégée to look to Islam which he did with a passion. He learned about various forms of Islam and became more radicalized along the way. He became enamored with the Hanafi movement led by Khaalis and the fundamentalist view of Islam that it represented. Khaalis gave him his new Islamic name, Dawud Salahuddin. The first name was the same as his son's who had been killed. The slaying of Khaalis's family further added to Salahuddin's radicalization.

Dawud Salahuddin, just a few short years from the hostage siege that Khaalis was leading would become infamous for his own actions. On July 22, 1980, Salahuddin, posing as a postman, went to the Bethesda home of Ali Akbar Tabatabai, who had been the press attaché at the Iranian Embassy prior to the Islamic Revolution. He was now serving as the press spokesman to have the Islamic Revolution overthrown restoring the Shah's family to power in Iran.

Tabatabai had received numerous death threats because of his work. A young medical student answered the door for him and the postman told him he needed for Tabatabai to sign for the letters. The student saw the uniform and the postal truck and became less concerned about the person at the front door. When Tabatabai came to the door, Dawud Salahuddin shot him three times and he died instantly. Salahuddin was able to escape Washington to Montreal, made his way to Geneva and eventually ended up in Tehran where, in his 60's, he still resides today.

Surely it was a horrendous crime that his family had endured and I recalled reading about the trial of the killers. As I lay on the 2nd floor landing, bleeding now for over a half an hour with my upper cheekbone busted up, piled up with my colleagues and being threatened with death, I remembered the article I read in 1974 in the *Philadelphia Inquirer.* I vividly recalled the headline and the article that described the crime and the trial.

I remembered and now I knew. I knew who this man was and I couldn't believe it.

I'm not a betting person—my wife would never give me enough allowance to bet–but I would have bet that no one else in that pile knew who was now addressing us and threatening to kill us. What I couldn't fully comprehend is why we were now being terrorized and threatened with death.

Khaalis ordered the gunmen who were with him on this level to shoot anyone who attempted to stand up. I would estimate that about a half hour or so had gone by and there was noise through stairwells and the police were now at the lobby level. The police must have tried to come up the stairs since Khaalis fired a number of shots down the stairs and the police backed off. Khaalis started screaming at the police that they had better back off or he would start to chop off heads and throw them over the railing. He yelled down to a policeman who was trying to talk to him and wanted to know if he was just an officer or someone in charge. The man said that his name was

Rabe. Khaalis asked him "What is your official title", he responded, "I am Deputy Chief Rabe. "Who are you?". Khaalis answered "You may call me Hamas Abdul Khaalis. " You can call me Mr. Khaalis and we will address each other formally while we talk to each other."

Khaalis then gave him a number and said "Call that number and they will give you instructions. You better stop that movie *Mohammad Messenger of God* by 2:00 pm or we will chop off 10 heads and throw them over the railing." He was furious because he felt the movie was blasphemous about the Prophet Mohammad and he wanted it stopped.

Based on what my colleagues and I were experiencing, I didn't doubt Khaalis's intentions and willingness to carry out his threats. I had never heard of the movie. To the best of my recollection, I had nothing to do with the movie nor did I think any of my associates had any connection to it.

At that moment, my only point of reference was knowing that Khaalis was profoundly upset that this movie was being shown in theaters. I didn't know who the movie was about, but based on the title, I could make an educated guess. If I made it out of this situation, I knew that I'd needed to learn more about the film.

CHAPTER TEN

MUSTAPHA AKKAD AND MOHAMMAD MESSENGER OF GOD

The movie concerned the birth of the Islam faith and the life of the Prophet Mohammad. It had been directed by Mustapha Akkad who was born in Syria and came to the United States to study film making at UCLA and the University of Southern California. He is best known for making the Halloween movies and _Lion of the Desert. Mohammad Messenger of God_ was the first movie he wanted to make in Hollywood but due to the film's potential controversy he was unable to find support to produce the film in the U. S.

It was originally being filmed in Morocco and had been supported by the rulers of Kuwait, Libya and Morocco. King Hassan II of Morocco had given his full backing and each country promised financial support. Six months into filming, the Saudi government exerted pressure on Morocco to stop the film. These political and religious difficulties stopped the filming. Akkad finally found a willing financial backer in Muammar al-Gaddifi the ruler of Libya; filming resumed and six months later was completed in Libya. It was made in both an English and Arabic version. In the English version Anthony Quinn stared as Hamza the Uncle of the Prophet and Irene Pappas stared as Hind who originally opposed Mohammad and had arranged for the killing of Hamza. When Akkad shot the film, a scene would be done in English and then re-shot with the actors in Arabic .

There are two distinct ironies about the movie and its connection to the terrorist siege that was just beginning to consume my colleagues and me. The first was the original release date of the movie—March 9, 1976, exactly one year to the date that we were now lying in a pile of men and women on the 2nd floor of the B'nai B'rith building. The second irony, and a sad one, is that Mustapha Akkad and his 34 year old daughter Rima Akkad Monla were killed on November 11, 2005 during a terrorist bombing. They were in the lobby of the Grand Hyatt in Amman, Jordan when an Al-Qaeda suicide bomber detonated his device. Akkad's daughter was killed instantly and he died a few days later from his injuries.

I'm not sure I can calculate the odds where a movie that was part of a terrorist act and potentially could be responsible for people losing their lives have the principal architect of the film killed by terrorism. One had to wonder whether the death of Akkad and his daughter was a matter of happen chance or was the making of the film in any matter connected? I don't know the answer but everyone I spoke with who heard the story found it difficult to comprehend that it was more than a coincidence. I sent an email to Malek Akkad, Mustafa Akkad's son who took over the family franchise of film making and in his own right a well respected film maker. My simple question was whether he thought his father and sister's deaths were connected to the movie? I did not receive an answer to my note.

CHAPTER ELEVEN

KHAALIS'S INITIAL DEMANDS AND THREATS OF DEATH

Khaalis also demanded the killers of his family be brought to him and that Mohammed Ali be brought to him as well. As I listened, I could understand the killers but I wasn't sure about Mohammed Ali? Later I learned he wanted Ali because he was a Black Muslim and close to Elijah Mohammed. He continued to repeat his demands and as I listened it occurred to me the killers of his family were not going to be delivered and that we would not be seeing Mohammed Ali. I truly thought we had a chance the movie would be stopped and I certainly hoped the authorities who now listening to his demands agreed.

He told the police that he was not going to stand around and let them stall— they better act quickly and they better do it right.

When Chief Rabe would call up and try to talk with him, sometimes Khaalis would talk, while other times he would say "don't you try to trick me these people's lives are at stake and you better just carry out the instructions". Nothing less would result in people being killed.

The gunmen with us on the 2nd floor landing seemed tremendously hyper. They were talking and chanting in an Arabic language in celebration of what they had accomplished to that point. Khaalis would say something and they would respond with a pride in their voices. They were also sharing smiles and nods of acknowledgement.

During this time, Khaalis began another tirade laced with anti-Semitic language. He emphatically informed us that this was a holy war, that he and his men were soldiers and that they were prepared to die in this holy war. He also emphasized that more civilians die in war than soldiers and that we should be prepared to die. He further instructed us that whoever we prayed to, we should pray to because we were going to die during this war. He alternately focused his attention on us and the police down the stairwell, every so often he would yell upstairs; communicating with someone on the floors above us, but not knowing which floors they were on.

More frequently he would yell up the stairwell and whoever was above would yell back. When this first started, he did not receive a reply back and the lack of response caused Khaalis to become agitated and concerned. If it was possible that even more tension could be created on the 2nd floor, it was quickly building among those of us piled on each other on that landing.

He picked a woman from the pile and told her to run up where his men were. She was given two minutes to return and let him know if his men were ok or he would start killing people. I took his threat to be serious and real and none of us were in a position to debate the issue with him. I wasn't sure who he had selected but I hoped she was a track star in school. I also hoped she would be able to keep her composure and fulfill the mission.

It was hard to discern what people were thinking and how they would react to specific commands and threats the terrorists might direct at a specific individual. Time seemed to be frozen. Khaalis's mantra kept up that he had better hear his men were ok, or people were about to die. After some time, Khaalis's men yelled down to him saying that they were alright and awaiting further instructions.

I estimated an hour had passed since we were in the piled on top of one another. We had been told to keep our heads down unless Khaalis told us to look at him and answer his questions with a yes sir. At one point he picked out a number of people, mostly women, to stand next to him by the elevators. A few of them were tremendously upset and emotional. They remained that way even after Khaalis and his men told them to calm down, but then threatened them with harm.

As they lined up, he asked each one their nationality. One was an Indian girl, and a number were black. He asked them why they were working with the Yehudi, a slang term for Jews, and didn't they know any better. He told them he was going to release them and had each one thank Allah for their freedom.

He also asked where the wounded man was. The pile of people was so high, he couldn't see where Wes was lying. He was told to get up and move towards Khaalis who then pointed towards the pile where I was situated along with Brian. Khaalis said "you, with the bloody face, get up and come over here." Brian and I both bleeding looked at each and neither of us made a move not knowing which one of us he wanted to join him. As we looked at each other it was almost like we were saying —please you go first, no you go first. If the situation was different, it would have been comical and we would have had a good laugh about it. Finally he described Brian's red shirt and Brian got up and was standing by the elevator near Wes.

It occurred to me at this point that if you were wearing a neck tie, which I was, you were perceived to be an executive with the organization and you were not going to be released no matter your physical condition. Too bad the casual nature of office attire that developed in America had not been in vogue in 1977. If everyone was dressed casually, that would have been a nightmare situation for Khaalis trying to figure out who was who.

Prior to releasing the women, Wes and Brian, Khaalis checked again to make sure his men were ok. He yelled to the police that he was sending more people down the stairwell and one was a wounded man. That was the last we saw of Wes and Brian.

At one point, with the police still close by in the stairwell, Khaalis decided that the 2nd floor landing was not very secure. He asked where the largest room was. Almost in unison we told him the 8th floor and he yelled up to his men about taking people to the 8th floor. The progression began, first from the 5th floor area and next from the 2nd floor landing.

This terrorist siege wasn't that far removed from the celebration of the Passover holiday in April which covers Moses leading the exodus of the Jewish people from the bondage of Egypt. Hamas Abdul Khaalis was now leading numerous people, the vast majority of them Jewish, from the freedoms they enjoyed to a bondage as hostages on the 8th floor of the B'nai B'rith building–a building that served as the launching point for programs and activities of a Jewish institution that stood for benevolence and compassion for all people.

At first, Khaalis told his men to take the women up the stairs to the 8th floor. They were gathered five or six at a time and told to stay close to each other as they went up the stairwells.

It was still very violent downstairs and if anyone did try to move or lift their head they were pushed down with gun butts; we were told that we would be shot if we didn't listen to their commands or tried to resist in any way. The men, as they sat up, were instructed to take off their neckties. One of the terrorists would take it and tie their hands behind their back, forcing their arms up as high as possible.

The men were sent upstairs no more than four at a time. As they were lined up, Khaalis was standing there warning them not to try anything funny because he was an excellent shot and would not hesitate shooting them with the pistol he was holding in his hand. Some of the men were questioned by Khaalis and he would verbally abuse them. It was always under the constant threat of death. We were carefully instructed that the men had to run up the stairs keeping close to the man in front and if there was any resistance or any move to try anything they would kill us in the stairwells.

Being on the bottom of the pile, I was in the last group of men taken from the 2nd floor to the 8th floor. I knew that I had been bleeding for over an hour. I wasn't sure how much blood I had lost and standing up, I quickly noticed how weak I felt. My legs were rubbery as well. Trying to steady myself, I took off my neck tie and waited for my hands to be tied. I'm sure other colleagues waiting in line had similar sensations. How could they not? In addition to feeling weak, there was also a feeling of total helplessness. Wondering if I'd make it up the six flights to the 8th floor. One of the terrorists tied my hands behind my back and pushed them up as high as they could go.

Ralph Janigan from accounting was standing in front of me and I knew that Sam Fishman from Hillel was standing behind me. Being in the last group was unsettling. The feeling of safety in numbers, though in reality this wasn't a highly rational thought, had disappeared. In the beginning the commotion on the 2nd floor produced a high volume of noise. At this moment, with just a few of us were standing in front of Khaalis and a couple of his henchmen, it was eerily quiet as he once again swore he would kill us if we tried anything funny. He motioned with his gun towards the stairwell and we were led to the door by one gunman armed with a semi automatic carbine rifle. He told us to start running up the stairs and added quickly that if any of us fell down in the stairwell he would just kill us and leave us there.

I was about to find out whether I'd make it up the six flights. You learn a lot about how your body reacts under stress and the physiological changes that can occur. The amount of adrenaline that my body began to produce probably would have allowed me to qualify for an Olympic sprint. The line, "we'll kill you in the stairs if you fall down", remained in my mind as we entered the stairwell. I wasn't sure if Ralph and Sam were prepared to run up the stairs, but I was. I recall pushing up against Ralph as we started to take some stairs two at a time and I felt Sam right behind me. I don't know the record time set that day from the 2nd floor to the 8th, but I'd bet we would be in the running for the top group. As we got to the top, the terrorist who escorted us said "You guys did a great job." and told us he was proud of us! He was proud of us! Can you believe it? He probably wanted me to say, "I've never felt so proud in my life for your compliment." That wasn't going to happen.

CHAPTER TWELVE

THE 8TH FLOOR
2:00 PM, WEDNESDAY, MARCH 9TH

As we got to the top and rounded the door, there was another gunman with a carbine rifle and machetes and knives around his neck waiting for us. He passed us to a tall thin gunman. Of all the gunmen I had encountered, this one was obviously the youngest. He was tall and was carrying a long gauge shotgun. He was wearing tan bicycle racing gloves that I found fascinating. This new terrorist was Abdul Hamid. Later, I tried to figure out why the bicycle racing gloves. They are cut off at the knuckles and don't impede one's ability to use one's fingers. It would have been difficult to pull the trigger of the shotgun if Abdul Hamid was wearing regular gloves. They truly came prepared in every way.

As I rounded the corner and Abdul Hamid instructed me where to go, never in my wildest dreams did I expect to see the scene I was taking in on the 8th floor. The unfinished conference room was three-quarters full of people, men and women, lying on their stomachs. If their hands had not been tied behind their backs, they had their hands extended straight out, holding on to the ankles of the person in front of them. The mass of humanity started from the back wall and went from side- to-side and filled most of the room. They made a place for us to lie down in the rows that were being formed and I was placed on the floor with Ralph Janigan on my left side and Sam Fishman on my right side. You could sense the fear and dread that existed the minute you came into the room. There were murmurings and many people were crying.

As on the 2nd floor, the scene seemed to be accentuated with color and sound. Perhaps my senses were in overdrive. At that point, I couldn't really concentrate on anyone since I was placed with my head towards the front of the room and the vast number of people were behind me.

Since the 8th floor was still under construction, the floor was hard cement— exactly what I needed. It looked like my prayer was answered and perhaps I wasn't going to bleed to death after all. I placed my face with the wound on the floor and pressed it as hard as I could to stop the bleeding. Since I was hit on the right side of my face, my head faced the elevator bank and the side of the floor that had been completed so I could observe what was happening in that area. I could feel Sam Fishman lying close to me.

Soon after being placed on the floor, I felt Sam wiping his eye and his face on my shoulder every so often. He obviously was trying to stop the bleeding from his eye. I'm sure Sam was having difficulty managing his own situation once they tied his hands behind his back with his neck tie. He could no longer hold his handkerchief up to his eye as he was doing on the 2nd floor landing where I thought that his eye had been taken out. As we lay close to one another, I heard Sam whispering to me, calling my name as if to ask me whether it was ok to wipe his face on my shirt. I was hopeful that he was getting some relief from using my shirt as a towel or soft bandage.

The terrorists seemed to be busy in the elevator area. They must have been getting their guns and supplies up to the 8th floor. Then Khaalis entered and began his first tirade at the entire group. He told us that Allah had answered his prayers for he had asked for 100 hostages and that he actually had more than that. The one disappointment Khaalis expressed was that he did not capture any of B'nai B'rith's senior professional and volunteer management. Dan Thursz, David Blumberg, B'nai B'rith's volunteer President, and Yale Goldberg, who was in charge of administrative matters at the organization, were offsite at a special gathering for Israel's Prime Minister Yitzhak Rabin, who was in Washington.

As events started to ignite, some initial concern among authorities was the attacks erupting around the city had a direct relation to the Prime Minister's visit. In terms of being thankful to a higher power, Khaalis and those of us now being held hostage were obviously on two different prayer tracks. Based on the situation, he obviously thought his faith in Allah was beneficial. For the more than 100 hostages now being held on the 8th floor of the B'nai B'rith building, we were trying not to lose faith.

As he spoke to us, he was once again covering the topics and grievances that he articulated to us on the 2nd floor landing. The anti-Semitic vehemence remained a major part of his diatribe. We, meaning the Jews, had created all the ills of the world. That they were soldiers and were prepared for their holy war. That more civilians died in war then soldiers and that whoever we prayed to, we should start praying. He mentioned the movie *Mohammad Messenger of God* and that we also better pray that the movie was being stopped or he would start killing people as he promised the police.

I remember looking at my watch when I first heard the loud noise in the building and told Harriet Berman that I'd go downstairs and see what was happening. It was about 11:00 am. There was no opportunity to have relooked at my watch from the moment I encountered the first terrorist. I was guessing that a few hours had passed and it was about 2:00 pm. I did know there was a huge disturbance in Washington. The constant sound of sirens was evident to us on the 8th floor. I thought the sounds of activity were directly related to what we were experiencing. I'm not sure at that particular moment I could have comprehended what was happening in our nation's capitol and what was in store for us in the hours to come.

After a short time, I was able to look over my left shoulder and notice other people in the room. I saw Al Elkes lying on his side. His hands were tied behind his back with his necktie like mine. His face was covered with soot and he looked like he was in some pain. I truly felt sad when I saw him—Al was such a gentle soul and wouldn't hurt anyone. He was an aficionado of theater. He loved to go to New York with his partner Eddie and friends to see shows. Al knew actors, actresses and directors from both New York and Hollywood and convinced many of his famous friends such as Joel Grey to join B'nai B'rith and then do public relations spots for the organization. He loved music. He proudly drove a black Oldsmobile Toranado that had AZE vanity plates that stood for Albert Z Elkes. It fully described him. I was sad for I wasn't sure how Al was going to handle the situation we were in. He looked directly at me and we both nodded and smiled at each other. It was as comforting as it could be under the circumstances.

Frances Bowie, who worked in the office services area, was a kind person who had that matronly aura about her and always inquired about your family. She looked at me and started to cry when she saw my face. I know she was expressing concern, although her reaction to what I looked like wasn't comforting at that time.

I saw Madeline Herman who worked in the public relations domain. We were close in age, had similar interests and had developed a friendship as colleagues. With my wife Jane and Madeline's husband (at the time) Ira we would get together as families for dinners. Madeline and Ira didn't have children at the time and enjoyed being around our daughter Emily. I think they were living parenthood vicariously through their interaction with Emily prior to having their first child a few years later.

I glanced at Nancy Steele who was Dan Thursz's secretary. She seemed incredibly upset and scared—emotions that were fully understandable under the circumstances. Her eyes were blackened from her mascara as she continued to cry.

Nancy had come to B'nai B'rith having worked for Dan previously. She never seemed happy, and I think her commute from Baltimore was a bit trying. If she had reservations about being at B'nai B'rith, as I looked at her, I'm sure her wisdom of being here was being questioned.

I saw Jerry Rudman being brought back into the 8th floor area; I'm not sure where they had him. He was still bleeding around his face as when I first saw him on the 2nd floor landing. He must have found his glasses since he was wearing them.

I also saw my colleague and friend Jay Manchester for the first time. Jay was Jerry's top assistant in the accounting area and we had developed a relationship soon after Jay arrived at B'nai B'rith. My wife Jane and I would see Jay and his wife Carol socially from time-to-time. During the day Jay and I would go out to lunch on a regular basis and compare notes about what was happening internally at the organization.

I finally noticed my assistant Harriet Berman. She looked ashen, and I was really concerned about her. She was single, in her 40's and her entire life revolved around her career as a professional secretary. She was always prim and proper–some might call her prudish. I'm sure her sensibilities were being challenged by the continuous vulgar language we were being exposed to.

I saw Norman Feingold who was the head of B'nai B'rith's career and counseling programs. Norman, a nationally known expert in his field had authored dozens of books and articles. He was lying behind me and he kept trying to talk to me and I kept quietly saying to him to be silent. The terrorists were agitated enough and they had told us they did not want us talking to one another.

I noticed many of the Anti-Defamation League staff including David Brody, ADL's Chief Washington lobbyist. It was said that David was the 101'st Senator having access to many members of congress and their staffs. The son of Russian garment workers, he received his law degree from Columbia University in 1940. He was short in stature but had a high level of intelligence that few could match. In addition to furthering Jewish causes, David was also a champion for civil rights in America. How ironic that at this very moment, David and his colleagues' civil rights were being denied and trampled upon.

I couldn't believe my eyes when I saw Dr. Bill Korey, B'nai B'rith's top international lobbyist. He had graduated from the University of Chicago in the mid 1940's and had received his graduate degrees from Columbia University. In 1960 he became head of B'nai B'rith's UN office and was an expert on ant-Semitism in Russia having authored numerous books on the subject. Bill was engaged in international issues on behalf of world Jewry that my simple mind had trouble comprehending. He now was also heading up B'nai B'rith's International Department and was splitting his time between New York and Washington. From a young staff person's perspective, David and Bill were at a level where you didn't approach them for casual conversation. They represented the elite of the B'nai B'rith staff. But now, they were just like the rest of us, wondering whether the person who now controlled our lives would carry out his threat of killing us all.

Also near me was Bernie Simon, the head of the organization's public relations office. However, I think he spent more time on an activity that was of greater interest to him and important to all staff members as the head of B'nai B'rith's pension plan. Bernie had originally joined the Anti-Defamation League staff in the mid 1940's and became part of B'nai B'rith in 1956. He authored hundred's of articles and also helped B'nai B'rith's former President and future Secretary of Commerce Phil Klutznick write a book. As I looked at Bernie I remembered an incident at the B'nai B'rith Convention in 1976 in Washington. I had a chance to work closely with him for the first time when a few of us were asked to develop position papers that were to be debated during workshops. Gun control was my assignment and I had a chance to work with experts from both perspectives. I believe that project allowed Bernie to develop some respect for me, in spite of my young age and experience, certainly in relation to what the senior level managers had accomplished with their lives.

One evening as we were walking down a hallway, Bernie was confronted by a volunteer member of the organization. They started screaming and cursing at each other and I did not have a clue as to what the issue was. He was threatening to get Bernie fired and Bernie told him to go ahead and try. Even with my nominal experience at that time, I instinctively knew that you just didn't get into what I was witnessing with volunteer leaders. After watching that, and it didn't seem to faze Bernie, I thought, wow that was impressive. I wasn't sure I'd ever have the gumption to do what Bernie just did. And now Bernie was lying near me with his hands tied behind his back with his necktie. We looked at one another and nodded. There was nothing else to do.

Also near me was Sidney Closter, who was the head fund raiser for the B'nai B'rith Foundation. A trained attorney, he received his law degree from The George Washington University after World War II. During the war, Sid had seen synagogues in Asia that had been destroyed and his initial fund raising experiences came from helping to restore those institutions. When you saw Sid in the office, he was constantly on the phone trying to raise money and chewing the ever present gum in his mouth. As we were lying there, I couldn't tell if Sid still had his gum.

Just a few feet away from me was Charlie Fenyvesi, the editor of B'nai B'rith's monthly magazine, the _National Jewish Monthly_. Since my first office at B'nai B'rith was on the same floor as the magazine's operations I got to know Charlie. I always admired his natty and preppy attire with a penchant for wearing bowties from time to time–something I could never pull off. I knew that Charlie had an incredible personal history. To me, he seemed to be quiet, studious and a nice man.

Born in Hungary, he had to live under a different name during the Holocaust. He and his parents survived the Holocaust, but numerous relatives were killed. After the 1956 revolution in Hungary, he came to the United States and was educated at Harvard. He received a Fulbright Fellowship and did work overseas.

As I looked at Charlie, it was difficult to comprehend what he was thinking and feeling. Here was a man who had experienced and survived the atrocities of the Holocaust. He had family members killed during the Holocaust and now was being subjected to this terrorist act steeped in anti-Semitic rhetoric (and all of us being threatened with death for the sheer fact that we were Jewish.) Was he quickly reliving aspects of his past that he had put in the recess of his mind that were now, rushing back as the waters from a glacier rush down a mountain?

There were others being held on the 8th floor that had grown up across Europe and had experienced the horrors of war and had personal experiences related to the Holocaust. I could not imagine how many of them were trying to deal with this situation. Charlie's eyes were mainly closed and when he opened them he noticed I was looking over at him and we nodded at one another. He also smiled at me.

Lying on the floor, it became easy to keep your eyes closed. It was a bit of a defense mechanism to try and blot out what was happening around you and when you re-opened your eyes the bad dream would be gone. Unfortunately, the reality of what was happening would come back quickly.

I saw David Leshnick for the first time. He worked within the Israel Affairs Committee. In 1975 we had offices next to each other and developed a relationship. David had long dark black hair and a full black beard and dark eyes to match. He spoke Hebrew and regularly traveled to Israel to work on programs, something that I was envied. (I did get my first trip to Israel in November 1975 for a young leadership mission that was sponsored by the National Jewish Federation.) His job at B'nai B'rith was to educate members about Israel and also encourage Aliah, the immigration of American Jews to live in Israel.

David was continually looking at me and shaking his head from side to side in a fashion to indicate no. I knew exactly what David was trying to say from across the room. He was indicating his strong feelings that we were going to die. When I would look back at David, I would gently shake my head up and down to indicate my feeling that everything was going to be ok. We did this head nodding back and forth for some time. I don't think he believed me at all and I'm not sure I believed myself. I felt it was worth the effort to continue to reassure David.

The terrorists began moving around the room specifically checking the men to see who was tied up and who had their hands free. There were a number of male colleagues who had not been bound up and many men and women were holding onto the ankles of the person in front of them. Since much of the 8th floor was under construction, the terrorists were finding a variety of materials including wire and rope that would be useful during the course of the event. These finds were helpful as they moved about the room. If a man had his necktie on, that was the binding of choice. They also started using the wire and rope to complete this part of their mission. Though the women were not tied up nor did they seem interested in doing so, they were cautious of this hands free situation.

At one point one of the terrorists thought that Rose Friedman, a secretary who worked for ADL, had untied David Brody. He went over to the area where David was located, pulled him up on his knees and hit him on the back of his head with his fist four or five times and retied his hands even tighter than they were. He told everyone that's what they'd get for not obeying orders. David had cried out when he was hit, obviously in pain. As I watched this spectacle, in addition to the apprehension and fear, there was an anger building in me as well. These guys thought they were brave, yet how brave was one for beating up a 50 year old man when he was defenseless.

The same thing happened to Bill Korey. One of the terrorists picked up Bill and dragged him from the middle of the room to a side wall. After moving him against the wall he hit him across the back with his rifle. Bill grimaced and groaned from taking the hit and as he was pushed back on the floor was told to be quiet.

I noticed my colleague Steven Morrison for the first time towards the back of the room off to the left. Soon after, I saw Steven being lifted up and placed with his head against the wall; his hands were tied behind his back. Whatever offense he had done in the terrorist's eyes, he was now standing there with his head against the wall and he looked uncomfortable and exposed. I thought perhaps he was talking to someone and they moved him out of the way so he couldn't talk.

I saw Si Cohen who headed up B'nai B'rith's Community Service efforts which were a large part of B'nai B'rith's work. When I came to B'nai B'rith's headquarters in Washington, Si was always available for a discussion as well as to offer advice and a kind word. Not far from Si was Dorothy Glaser, Si's assistant. They had a close personal relationship and she watched him constantly with a look of concern.

At about this time, I glanced back at Charlie Fenyevesi. His look had changed considerably; he was ashen and his eyes were rolling back in his head. He started talking to himself and he was getting louder. He almost shouted out and said the following:-"You guys can't keep me here any longer and I'm going to leave you now." As he said this, he was trying to get up, but that would have been an impossible feat to pull off considering he was prone and his hands were tied behind his back. I couldn't tell if Charlie was hallucinating and it was related to his experiences from his youth or he was suffering from some kind of medical occurrence. It became obvious as the seconds went by that Charlie was starting to suffer from a diabetic shock and he was going from a conscious state to one of passing out. A few of the women near Charlie started screaming that he was sick and needed help. They pleaded with the terrorists to give him something sweet to eat.

A few minutes later, miraculously, an orange appeared and from where I don't know. The women who were untied were passing the orange from person to person to get it closer to Charlie. It hit the floor a few times during its journey across the room. As it got to Charlie, Khaalis had come back into the room and said "don't feed that orange to that man." A few of the women started screaming that he was going to die unless they could give him some orange. Khaalis quietly stated, "That orange is dirty. You can't feed that dirty orange to that man. It has to be washed off first."

Nancy Steele was near Charlie. She was looking a bit better than she had a few hours ago. She offered to wash off the orange which they let her do. When she returned, she slowly fed the orange to Charlie. Soon after, he looked like he was feeling better and was quietly sleeping. Clearly a crisis where one of our colleagues perhaps could have died was averted.

As I looked at Charlie, he was sleeping now and seemed more at peace then he did just a few short minutes ago. I wondered why would the terrorists go to some lengths to locate something sweet to give to Charlie if they were going to kill us? There were other instances when a number of colleagues started to complain about chest pains or other ailments and they mentioned to the terrorists that they had their medication in their pockets. After looking at the medication, they allowed a number of people to take them.

As I thought about these actions, it occurred to me that the terrorists did not want anyone to die of natural causes. It also occurred to me that if Khaalis told the police he was sending down the body of someone who had died on the 8th floor the reaction, and any plans the police were contemplating, probably would have had to be re-evaluated. If you were the police and thought people were dying, what would you do? I would think that I didn't have a lot of time to let this go on and would need a plan to free the hostages.

At the start of the siege, no one was called out by name. The terrorists were not engaging in conversation with anyone and they certainly didn't stop to inquire what our names were. So it was surprising when Khaalis came from the other side of the 8th floor and asked who David Brody was. No one said anything and no one wanted to let him know where David was. Finally David called out that he was David Brody. Khaalis made his way through everyone lying on the floor stepping through lines of people to get up right next to him. A few of the women softly cried out for Khaalis not to hurt David. He now stood right above David and quietly said, "Mr. Brody, knowing presidents will not help you now." Khaalis had obviously seen David's office where he proudly displayed pictures of him with every U.S. President since Truman that had been personally signed with a nice salutation to him. Khaalis then quickly turned and walked out of the room. His point to the group was well taken. It was a firm and undeniable affirmation that he was in charge and he was going to make decisions about our lives. It didn't matter whom we knew; it didn't matter what we did or what our status in life was. Hamas Abdul Khaalis would be the decider of life and death.

The tension on the 8th floor was incredible. There were a number of large windows facing Rhode Island Avenue. Across the street was a Holiday

Inn and right next to it, the Gramercy Inn which had a nice restaurant and was a favorite hangout for B'nai B'rith staff to have lunch. It was convenient and the food was pretty good.

Al Elkes and Harold Brenner took me to lunch when I came into Washington for my interview to join B'nai B'rith at the end of 1973. Little did I know that one of our favorite lunch hang outs would become one of the police tactical operation centers since it was conveniently located right next door. Directly behind the building was a beautiful old brick office building that later was turned into a school. Diagonal from the B'nai B'rith Building a new YMCA was under construction. The terrorists became concerned about the windows facing Rhode Island Avenue. They thought that the police had already taken up positions across the street on the roof of the Holiday Inn and that snipers were looking into the building, targeting them. At one point, a terrorist called over Jay Manchester to the windows. The terrorist told him that he was going to "string him up, upside down to give the police sharp shooters something to shoot at." They also took a few other men from the floor, prior to tying them up, to help them cover up the windows. Some of the materials the terrorists found left over from the construction crew included a variety of cardboard, brown paper and different paints. A number of colleagues were busying themselves putting up the brown paper and cardboard and painting the windows. One colleague must have gotten a can of some kind of clear primer because as he worked feverishly, nothing seemed to be happening. He was painting and painting and the window was not being covered up. One of the terrorists finally admonished him and asked him what exactly he was doing. He finally found a paint can that had real paint and he began to coat the window.

As work proceeded covering the windows, young men who were under 30 were told to call out. The terrorists had decided they needed laborers and there was ample free labor at their disposal. They didn't explain why, though the young men on staff were about to serve on work crews in hard labor for extended hours. The analogous situation of forced labor that occurred at Nazi death camps was not lost on me.

As young men were calling out, men over 50 were told to identify themselves. They were grouped together and their hands were untied. They were told they were going to be the first to die since they had already lived their lives and be prepared to have their heads cut-off. As I looked

61

at my colleagues in this age group over by the windows area, I was trying to imagine what they were thinking. They now had been anointed by the leader of the terrorists and singled out for their lives to end. If they were terrified by this prospect, their actions did not outwardly show their fear or dread. Perhaps, as with many people now being held on the 8th floor, they were quickly working through the realization that the prospect of being killed was real and in their own private mind they were coming to terms with what was happening.

The older men were instructed to help the younger men stand up since their hands were tied behind their backs. Once standing younger men selected by the terrorists were taken to a holding area near where I was lying.

One of the first over was Jay Manchester, who quietly asked me if I was okay. I could see in Jay's eyes that he was frightened and trying to size-up what was happening. He was down on one knee and was concentrating on the terrorists. He looked like he was ready to spring into action at any second. I'm sure he was experiencing an adrenaline rush but I'm not sure he was aware of it. He looked focused and like most of us was processing what our senses were telling us.

We were in a very difficult situation and the information our eyes and ears was sending to our brains was changing rapidly. I don't think the terrorists were following a particular script except perhaps what they had planned prior to the takeover of the building. They seemed to be improvising as the seconds were adding to minutes and now the minutes since the siege began had turned into hours. Jay's simple question to me, in spite of what I know was his own fear and uncertainty, was truly and deeply appreciated. I know he was concerned about my appearance and the severity of my injury. Such simple acts of kindness would play out among colleagues throughout the entire event.

The terrorists continued to tell young men to yell out and I did as well. The one whom I had identified as the youngest terrorist when I came into the 8th floor, Abdul Hamid, kicked me in my legs to get up. At this point I was still bleeding fairly heavily from my wound and as I started to try and get up, I turned my head to the right and we looked at each other. His comment to me was, "Man, get back down, your face is way too messed up." Though his actual comment was way more vulgar than the quote I just offered. I have to admit, at this stage and still feeling weak, I was happy to comply with his missive. I lied back down and continued to press my face against the floor, applying pressure to stop the bleeding. Meanwhile more of my younger colleagues were being gathered in the holding area.

During the initial time we were being held on the 8th floor, Khaalis continued to come in and out of the area. He was spending time over in the completed section of the floor where the new offices of ADL were located. He was in the process of setting up the area which would serve as his command center.

Prior to being moved to the 8th floor, when we first encountered Khaalis, he inquired about bathroom facilities and water on that level. Both existed where he would be taking everyone. Standing in front of the entire group, in addition to continuing his ant-Semitic comments, Khaalis went through a rather lengthy discourse on cleanliness. Men had to go to the bathroom like Muslims, sit down on the toilet like women to make sure that everything is very clean before and after the process. There was a men's and ladies' bathroom and Khaalis designated the men's room as his and his men's facility and everyone else was to use the ladies' bathroom. Anyone who entered the terrorists designated facility would be killed. Prior to Khaalis and his men using the men's room, one of my colleagues was sent to insure it was clean for the terrorist's usage. Soon after, a number of women began asking to use the bathroom. The terrorists indicated they could go two at a time. The women were allowed to line up and the line started near the area of the elevators and made its way back to the end of the room. The scene was typical of those repeated everyday at such venues as the Kennedy Center, sports stadium or any place else in America where women have to line up constantly to use the restroom. Just because we were being held hostage why should it be any different when it came to women and restrooms?

Khaalis told the women they would be treated with respect and they had nothing to worry about. He told them all of the terrorists had wives or girlfriends who were beautiful and they did not have to satisfy their desires, particularly with Jewish women. As he told them they would be treated with respect, I guess that respect did not start with the violent takeover of the building. Many of my colleagues who were women were hit with weapons, punched, kicked, had their hair pulled and were forced to lie in the piles of people the terrorists had made on the 2nd, 5th and 6th floors. They were threatened with death constantly. If you were to ask the women who were now being held against their will on the 8th floor if they felt respected and safe, I would have bet the ranch they didn't feel respected. At least they made no effort to tie up all the women. I truly believe that if the terrorists felt the women were going to be a threat to their own safety, they would have been tied up just as the men were.

It was about this time that Khaalis had come back into the section of the 8th floor where we were being held to solicit help in getting the phone's to work. We had installed a new Centrex phone system a few months before that never worked properly and I found it funny that he couldn't figure out how to make an outside call. He was annoyed and obviously frustrated.

When it came to the new phone system that was installed by management, he wasn't alone. The entire staff had the same feeling–it was impossible to work. Supposedly it was state of the art available. The one thing we could agree on with Hamas Abdul Khaalis was the B'nai B'rith phone system.

He asked who knew how to work it and no one answered. He asked a number of times and each time he was more annoyed there was no response. Finally, Betty Jean Neal (BJ) from our human resources department, who was sitting with her back against the wall told him that she'd answer his damn phones. If there was anyone on staff who had the nerve to answer him, it was BJ. I think that she thought no one else was going to respond to his demand and that someone needed to do it and it might as well be her. In reality, BJ said she couldn't believe that it was her voice answering and what was she thinking? For a moment the two of them were just staring at each other. It seemed like Khaalis was looking at her in amusement. Perhaps he recognized the woman that he had kicked in the face just hours earlier when he had told her to get up. Her glasses had slipped off and she went to get them. He kicked her on the chin. She had looked up afterwards and told him, "Damn it, I was just getting my glasses."

He finally asked her name and she told him. He then asked if she was Jewish and she said no. He indicated that he was glad that she was not Jewish since he didn't want any Jewish bitches answering his phone. On this point, a number of us have different recollections. I recall him saying "Jewish bitch" and BJ remembers "Jewish bastards." Either way, it was obvious he was happy that the person who knew how to work the fickle Centrex phone system was not Jewish. I don't think that BJ ever thought she'd be able to place on her resume that she served as the secretary and administrative assistant for the leader of a terrorist siege. He told her to follow him, and she disappeared around the wall by the elevator bank and we were not to see BJ again for more than 36 hours.

The terrorists became concerned the men and women were still mixed together lying on the floor and finally decided to separate them. The women were placed along the wall of windows which were now covered up. The terrorists left open a small space in the windows to see what was happening along the Rhode Island Avenue side of the building where police snipers had most likely been situated.

The men were pushed towards the opposite side of the room. Those not considered over 50 and those young men who had been drafted to serve on work crews and were now tied up with either their neckties or rope from the construction work.

The terrorists now concentrated on organizing the work crews. As they consolidated the building, bringing more than 100 people to the 8th floor, they also brought the elevators up to the 8th floor and cut them off. They still had a major concern about the stairwells that started at the bottom of the building and went all the way up to a door that led up to the roof. In spite of their weapons, ammunition and advantage of knowing what was happening in the building—which the police didn't, they were concerned about their vulnerability with the stairwells.

It was probably mid-afternoon when the young men on the B'nai B'rith staff were put to work. They started on the lower floors and the plan was fairly simple though the execution of it was not. They were forced to literally take the B'nai B'rith building apart. They went into offices on each floor and moved anything that was not nailed down— desks, chairs, filing cabinets and tables—into the stairwells. Those of us not involved on work crews could hear the noise their work created. The terrorists were screaming and exhorting the young men to work harder and faster and those demands never ceased. I wasn't sure what floors they were on but the noise was loud. You could hear metal crashing as large and small objects were thrown down the stairwells.

In addition to furniture and other materials, the work crews were told to throw down construction materials as well. These included ladders, paint cans and other loose materials. It never actually occurred to me that many of the items being added to the stairwell consisted of highly flammable material. They were creating a situation where the B'nai B'rith Building was becoming a tinderbox that only needed a match to become an inferno.

As young staff members were working, Khaalis's men also had them help cover the windows where his command center was now located. They were also placing desks and other office furniture around the windows to try and block all site lines the police might have been looking for.

The work crews were also creating further anxiety for those individuals hidden in offices throughout the building who had not been captured during the initial moments of the siege. It allowed the terrorists to check again on offices and try doors that were locked or had furniture piled up against them. These colleagues tried to remain quiet as the day wore on, wondering what might happen to them. They were also afraid to pick up their phones. A line light might appear on a phone outside of their office that would signal where they were. Although not being directly held and threatened, they were hostages as well. Completely in the dark, they did not know why the building was attacked and who was responsible. There were also a number of staff members who were completely alone–left with their individual thoughts and fears. I'm sure they were hearing the noises in the building and stairwells but had no idea what they meant. For many, I'm sure they thought the gunmen they saw or had heard about were finally coming for them as well.

From the beginning of the siege another constant noise we heard came from outside the building–the wailing of police sirens and emergency vehicles and the drone of helicopters. The din was steady and uninterrupted from the time I was on the 2nd floor landing until now being on the 8th floor.

What we didn't realize at this juncture was the B'nai B'rith Building was not the only site for terrorist activity that day. The gravity of the situation was far worse than we or the police authorities could have imagined.

CHAPTER THIRTEEN

A CITY UNDER SIEGE

When Khaalis took BJ around the corner, he told her to sit at a desk at the front of the room on the Rhode Island Avenue side. He took a chair, sat across from her and told her to write down a series of phone numbers. One was for his house on 16ᵗʰ Street, the other for Deputy Chief Rabe. He also gave her three separate numbers for the Islamic Center situated on Massachusetts Avenue.

The first call was to Khaalis's home. A voice answered and BJ explained she was Mrs. Neal from the B'nai B'rith Building and that Mr. Khaalis wanted to speak with them. Khaalis told them that Allah had answered his prayers for more than 100 people had been captured and were hostages. He said he also prayed that Dr. Rauf, head of the Islamic Center, would be captured.

After he hung up, he had BJ call the Islamic Center. At about the same time the B'nai B'rith Building was attacked, three of Khaalis's followers took over the Islamic Center. Brothers Abdul Rahim, Abdul Rahman and Abdul Al Qawee entered the Islamic Center. They confronted Dr. Rauf about his support of the Black Muslim movement and that Egypt, his country of birth, was in the process of trying to arrange peace with the Jews. Dr. Rauf and others were taken as hostages.

The call to the Islamic Center was answered by Rahman and BJ told him Khaalis wanted to speak with him. At that point, Khaalis learned that Dr. Rauf and his wife had been captured. He told his men to remain cool and calm and that Dr. Rauf would be killed. He gave the phone back to

67

BJ and had her give the gunmen all seven extensions on the phone in front of her. He took the phone back and further instructed his men to refer any calls to the numbers they had just been given.

While BJ was making calls for Khaalis, Abdul Adam was in front of the elevators with what looked like a boom box. It was some kind of radio that he was listening to. I don't know if they had brought it with them or he had found it in one of the offices. My location on the floor allowed me to hear the radio and what the terrorists were discussing.

This is when I learned the attack on the B'nai B'rith building was one of a number of coordinated attacks that had occurred around the Washington area by Khaalis and his followers.

I heard the District Building being mentioned, which I knew was the seat of the District of Columbia's government and also something about an Islamic Center. I didn't know much about the Islamic Center except it was a beautiful edifice located on Massachusetts Avenue near the turnoff to Rock Creek Parkway. I thought it had been funded by the Shah of Iran.

As the attacks on the B'nai B'rith Building and Islamic Center were proceeding, Abdul Muzikir and Abdul Nuh, two other followers of Khaalis, went to the District of Columbia Council chambers looking for high-level District officials to capture. Not finding any, they took 15 hostages—an assortment of people who by fate were in a location that was about to become extremely violent. The two terrorists had a shotgun, ammunition and machete with them. Mack Cantrell, a security guard, approached the doors of the Council Chamber and Abdul Muzikir fired the weapon. Cantrell was hit in the face and seriously wounded. He did not die from the wound, but a short time later died of a heart attack. It is hard not to believe the serious wounds he received did not contribute to his early demise.

Marion Barry, a DC Council member at the time and future Mayor of Washington, was getting off an elevator on the floor and took a shotgun pellet that lodged in his chest near his heart.

A young reporter, Maurice Williams who worked for Howard University's radio station WHUR, was also getting off an elevator on that floor and took shotgun pellets in his chest. He died where he fell.

As police arrived on the 5th floor they exchanged gunfire and during this period, the terrorist shot one of the hostages, Robert Pierce, in the back while he lied on the floor. The wound instantly paralyzed him. As I listened carefully, I could hear that a young news reporter had been killed at the District Building. I didn't pick up what had happened to Marion Barry or the hostage Robert Pierce. At that point, Abdul Adam walked away from the elevator bank and headed towards Khaalis' command center.

I'm not sure any of my colleagues heard what I had just heard. I now knew there were other buildings involved and that someone had been killed, though I did not know who. Hearing the radio and processing this information did not alleviate my anxiety about the situation. If anything, it heightened my sense that our plight was even more serious and dangerous.

When Adam walked back to Khaalis, he wanted him to hear what was coming over the radio. BJ indicated the three of them listened to a news channel and heard the report about the District Building take over and the killing that had occurred. Now there were three. The B'nai B'rith building, the Islamic Center and the District Building.

Later that Wednesday afternoon, Khaalis came into the room for a short time and announced proudly to all of us that his men had succeeded in their endeavor. He boasted that people had not listened to him and now they would. As he made his pronouncements, all of his men were gathered in the room—Abdul Latif, Abdul Adam, Abdul Salaam, Abdul Razzaaq, Abdul Shaheed and Abdul Hamid. They would confirm his thoughts as he made them and would say Islamic phrases in unison to celebrate what they considered their victory.

CHAPTER FOUTEEN

8ᵀᴴ FLOOR, WEDNESDAY, MARCH 9TH

The work crews continued their efforts throughout the afternoon. The mood and situation on the 8th floor was like a wild roller coaster ride. There would be brief periods of respite from the anti-Semitic tirade and then hyper- activity from the terrorists if they noticed movement by the police. At one point, one of the terrorists was looking through the small opening they had left and truly became agitated. He started screaming he saw sharp shooters being positioned on the roof across the street. He quickly made his way towards Khaalis.

When Khaalis was informed of the police action, he told BJ to get the police on the line. She called the general number for police in the District and told them who she was, that she was at the B'nai B'rith Building and it was an emergency. She wasn't sure who she was connected to, but gave them one of the numbers to call back on and asked that they do so immediately.

While waiting for the call back, Khaalis told BJ to get the District Building on the phone. With the chaos happening at there, it took all of BJ's creativity to figure out how to connect with someone. She finally reached an operator, explained who she was and that she needed to speak to Khaalis's men. When finally connected, Khaalis told his man to remain cool and calm and asked for a number at the District Building where Khaalis could call him.

Khaalis then received a call back from Deputy Chief Rabe. He told the Chief he knew about the sharp shooters on the roof across the street and if they shot into the building, they would be killing the hostages who would be placed in front of the windows–his men would not be killed. Chief Rabe told Khaalis the sharp shooters would be removed.

As the day wore on, the terrorists placed two guards to watch us in the 8th floor area. They put two chairs on opposite sides of the room and the terrorists rotated among themselves. They would sit in the chairs with their rifles and shotguns across their laps and tell us to keep quiet, constantly reminding us that we were going to die in the holy war they started. The two who drew the first watch were Abdul Latif and Abdul Salaam. I was convinced that Latif was the 2nd in command to Khaalis. Salaam had on a hat that one would describe as floppy for it allowed him to pull it down over his forehead and be close to his eyes.

The line for the ladies room remained active throughout Wednesday afternoon. It wasn't until later that afternoon that they decided to let men use the bathroom as well. The difference in the procedure was like two different universes. The men could only go one at a time. The way you were tied up, it was very difficult to try and stand on your own. This is where the older men, who were untied and would be the first to die, came into the act. If you couldn't stand up on your own, one of the older men—as defined by the terrorist– would try and assist you.

The few hours that had now passed involved huge physical and emotional turmoil. No one on staff had any food or water and people were feeling weaker than they felt at 11:00 am. It was not easy for the older staff members to help lift dead weight. It was an arduous task they would have to assist with for some time to come. Getting to your feet was just the first phase for the men. Next you proceeded across the room, with your hands still tied behind your back. One of the terrorists waited for you by the wall near the hall way where the bathrooms were located, diagonally across from the elevators. Your head was placed against the wall at a 45 degree angle with all the pressure on your neck. The terrorist would put his rifle or shotgun into your neck or head while they untied your hands. This was accompanied by verbal abuse that was similar to what I originally heard on the 2nd floor landing and continued with Khaalis on the 8th floor. The Jews created all the ills of the world, that we should go back to where we came from; and that as Jews we didn't deserve to live.

I don't recall who was the first man to test out the trials and tribulations of going to the restroom, but I watched with interest. The experience did not seem very pleasant. When I watched the terrorist place the rifle in the neck of my colleague, I wondered if the safety was on and how easy would it be for the gun to fire, even accidentally. I determined at that point on Wednesday afternoon that I would hold off as long as humanly possible. I already felt dehydrated and didn't need the men's room. Witnessing the spectacle in front of me, further convinced me my decision was a wise one.

CHAPTER FIFTEEN

ZAHEDI, YAQUB-KHAN AND GHORBAL. THE SIEGE BECOMES INTERNATIONAL

The police were dealing with three siege fronts in the city. They did not know exactly how many terrorists were involved or how heavily armed they might be. The terrorists obviously had guns since shots had been fired at them and a few people who had suffered gunshot wounds were released. They also knew that four people were wounded, one fatally and three seriously at the District Building. What they did not know was how many terrorists were involved and how many weapons they had. Based on their reaction to Alton Kirkland crawling out of the elevator that afternoon, they were concerned the terrorists might have explosives. Khaalis was known to the police from the murder of his family and since he was at the B'nai B'rith Building they were assuming this location was going to be a central point. As Wednesday progressed, the police, FBI and other government agencies were trying to figure out a plan of action in trying to manage a major terrorist incident in the United States.

Some determination was made by law enforcement officials that with Khaalis's Islamic background and fervency, it would be best to reach out to experts on Islam to see if there might be any openings that could help them deal with him. Washington, being the home of numerous embassies, many of them representing Islamic countries, meant there were experts close by. Through conversations between District Police, FBI and now the State Department, contact would be made.

One such call went to Ardeshir Zahedi, Ambassador to the United States from Iran. The call was made by Ambassador Armin Myer. Meyer had been Ambassador to Lebanon from 1961 – 1965, Ambassador to Iran from 1965 – 1969 and Ambassador to Japan from 1969 – 1972. After his Ambassadorship to Japan, he returned to the State Department in Washington in 1973 where he headed a new task force to study international terrorism. It had been created by President Richard Nixon after the murder of the Israeli athletes at the Munich Olympics. Ambassador Meyer decided to call his friend Ardeshir Zahedi. He hunted down Zahedi who was visiting a friend in Nice, France who was ill with cancer.

Ambassador Zahedi was 48 years old and was the Shah's former son-in-law having married the Shah's daughter in 1959 though they were divorced in 1964. In spite of the divorce, Ambassador Zahedi remained close to the Shah having served as Foreign Minister of Iran in the early 1960's as well as Ambassador to the Court of St. James and now was Iran's Ambassador to the United States. He was well liked and respected as Iran's representative in Washington and had developed relationships and friendships with America's political elite and celebrities. Zahedi hosted numerous affairs that people constantly worked at to be invited and to be seen. He was very generous towards many charities and people appreciated these efforts.

Ambassador Meyer briefed him on what was happening in Washington and asked him to return as quickly as possible. The Ambassador also received a call from President Carter urging his assistance. As he was briefed on the situation in Washington, he quickly understood the seriousness of the situation and that people's lives were at stake. Ambassador Zahedi did not consider himself to be a religious person, but he felt something was pulling and leading him to act. He had a conviction that his willingness to become involved could actually save lives. Since France was six hours ahead of Washington, Ambassador Zahedi used the time difference to his advantage. He asked his embassy staff in Washington to contact the foreign ministry of France to help make travel arrangements. He also asked for one of his aides who was much more knowledgeable about the Koran and its verses to be prepared to meet him upon his return. Not being a religious man, he understood his limitations in this area. A short time later, the Ambassador had a conversation with France's President Valery Giscard d'Estaing in arranging for a private plane to take him from Nice to Paris. A seat on the Concorde would be waiting for him to get him to Dulles Airport in half the time it would normally take to cross the Atlantic.

The Ambassador was back in Washington by about noon on Wednesday, March 9th, and went immediately to his embassy. He also understood and appreciated the potential international and diplomatic ramifications of his involvement. After his conversation with Ambassador Meyer, he placed a call to his King, the Shah of Iran. He reached the Shah's office and spoke with one of his aides. The aide informed him the Shah was not available having left for the airport to catch a flight. Ambassador Zahedi told him it was imperative that he speak with his King. He told the aide he would wait on the line while he tried to locate the Shah. The aide finally informed the Ambassador he had located the Shah at the airport and would connect them. Ambassador Zahedi briefed his King on what he knew of the events in Washington. People's lives were in danger and thus the call for his assistance. During their conversation, Ambassador Zahedi told his King if his involvement in any way would cause difficulty for the Shah or for Iran, he would immediately resign his Ambassadorship and help as a private citizen. He said to the Shah that if authorities felt he could help save lives, he needed to assist and participate. The Shah informed him it would not be necessary to resign his Ambassadorship and he would be involved as the Ambassador of Iran to the United States.

In addition, Ambassador Zahedi reached out to Ambassador Yaqub-Khan from Pakistan and Ambassador Ghorbal of Egypt. Yaqub-Kahn was 56 years old, a retired Lt. General of the Pakistan Army and a former Chief of Staff. Ambassador Yaqub-Kahn had served with the British Indian Army during World War II. He had been captured twice and escaped twice. He was an internationally recognized polo player and had a knack for languages being fluent in English, French, German, Italian, Russian and Urdi.

Ghorbal, 51 years old, was slight of statue *being about 5 feet tall,* but with a big brain obtaining Master's and Doctoral degrees from Harvard. He had served his country in Paris, Geneva, London and Ottawa. Both agreed to help. Ambassador Zahedi had been engaged in situations involving both of their countries and knew both men on a personal basis. He was involved in discussions to help relieve tensions between Pakistan and India as well as India/China relations which had tremendous consequences for Pakistan. He was closer to Ambassador Ghorbal serving as a go between for Israel and Egypt on numerous matters prior to and up to the peace treaty that Israel and Egypt signed. When Ambassador Zahedi was Foreign Minister of Iran, he was the only Foreign Minister within the Islamic community that developed close personal relationships with Israeli leaders. He knew all the political leaders from the inception of the State of Israel including David Ben-Gurion, Moshe Dyan, Yitzhak Rabin, Shimon Peres, Golda Mier and Abba Eban. He told his fellow Ambassadors that he was in the process of getting back to Washington and they would arrange to meet at the Iranian Embassy. He also suggested they call their leaders, Bhutto of Pakistan and Sadat of Egypt, to gain their approval to help.

CHAPTER SIXTEEN

PATRICK MULLANY

On a parallel track, discussions were going on within the structure of the FBI on who needed to be involved and would be helpful in dealing with the events that were starting to overtake Washington. Jim Adams was serving as Associate Director of the FBI, the number two person to Director Clarence Kelley. He decided to call Agent Patrick Mullany. Mullany was considered one of the premier terrorism and hostage experts within the FBI. He was one of four individuals who had developed skill sets and knowledge about a specialty area that was truly in its infancy. Howard Teten, Tom Strentz and Conrad Hassel joined Patrick Mullany as the FBI experts. The concept of hostage negotiation was just beginning in the mid-1970's and many in the FBI looked at the emerging discipline with a jaundiced eye.

The idea of behavioral assessment and hostage negotiation as a law enforcement tool was formulated in New York City by Lt. Frank Boltz and psychologist Harvey Schlossberg. They developed a class at the Police Academy in New York and had invited Patrick Mullany and Howard Teten to lecture on abnormal behavior.

Adams called Mullany, who was in Cleveland, Ohio, handling a tense hostage negotiation that had just concluded. Corey Moore, a former Marine, finally released the two hostages he held for 46 hours–Shelley Ann Kiggans and police Captain Leo Keglovic. This was one of a few individual hostage situations that occurred in 1977. One other case he handled that year was in Indianapolis, Indiana where a mortgage banker was held with a shotgun tied around his neck. It received wide national coverage.

When Mullany received the call from Adams, he could not have realized he was about to utilize his skills and knowledge in a situation he and his colleagues never encountered before. Mullany jumped into a patrol car and with lights and siren going, rushed to Cleveland's airport for a flight to Washington. The United flight's doors were closed and the ramp was being pulled back. The uniformed police officer running with Mullany to the plane yelled at the agent to get the ramp back and get the plane door reopened. The pilot complied and Patrick Mullany was now safely on the plane for Washington. Though the information he received was fairly thin as he sped to the airport, he sensed he was headed towards a major hostage situation.

CHAPTER SEVENTEEN

THE MEDIA GETS INVOLVED

Back in Khaalis's 8ᵗʰ floor command center, he was receiving a variety of calls on the seven lines that BJ was handling. When she needed to answer a line, she had to make a note of what call was coming and who was on the line so she wouldn't become confused and Khaalis could decide whether he wanted to take the call. Late Wednesday afternoon when she answered the phone the caller asked "BJ is that you?" She recognized the voice–David Blumberg, President of B'nai B'rith. He asked if she was ok. Always respectful, she said, "I'm ok, Mr. Blumberg." Inquiring about other staff members, she told him she wasn't with her colleagues. He then asked to speak with Khaalis. She turned to Khaalis and said, "Mr. Blumberg, the President of B'nai B'rith, wants to speak with you." Khaalis said, "Tell that Jew Bastard that I don't want to speak with him and then hang up." BJ said to Khaalis, "I could never tell Mr. Blumberg that." Khaalis insisted that she tell him that exactly. So she said to David, "Mr. Khaalis said he didn't want to speak with you." and she hung up the phone. Khaalis was annoyed with BJ and wanted to know why she didn't tell him what he said. She just reiterated that she could never say that to Mr. Blumberg.

About the same time Blumberg called, BJ took another call. There was a young male voice asking to speak with his mother. Being in human resources, BJ knew about the personal lives of all the B'nai B'rith employees–good and bad–who worked in the building and she knew what this call was about. Every day at about this time a young boy called his mother to let her know that he was home from school. Khaalis told BJ that if any calls came in that he most likely did not want to speak with she was to tell them the building was closed and hang up. That's what BJ told the young caller. A few minutes later, a line rang and when BJ answered it was the boy asking to speak with his mother. BJ again told him the building was closed and she hung up. A very short time later she picked up a line and for the third time it was the young boy telling her that he needed to speak with his mother, that she was a mean lady and that if she didn't let him speak with his mother, he was going to call the police.

BJ's instant response to the boy which matched her sense of humor and irony of life, was please do! She then hung up. That's exactly what the boy did–called the police to complain about the mean lady at the B'nai B'rith building. The police noted where he lived and sent a squad car to be with him until relatives could be located.

Though my colleagues and I were in a critical situation with our lives in danger, this might have been easier to handle than the thoughts going through the minds of loved ones. They could only conjure up horrible images not knowing whether loved ones were alive or dead. I always realized that at least I knew what was happening here and could try and deal with the situation. I imagine that many of my colleagues were trying mental telepathy that would somehow deliver a message to their loved ones on their current state. Perhaps it would have been somewhat comforting.

As the afternoon wore on, many of the incoming calls were from the press. One of the first calls BJ fielded was from Max Robinson an anchor on Channel 9, the CBS affiliate, who also did news for WTOP radio. (Robinson would go on to be the first black newscaster to do national news for ABC. He tragically died of AIDS some years later). Khaalis was eager to speak with the press and go over his demands and complaints. As Khaalis spoke with Robinson, he had BJ write a number down where Robinson could be reached.

At the beginning and throughout the siege, news reports about what was going on at the three buildings was continuously updated. Stations interrupted regularly scheduled programs to provide the latest details. This also allowed Khaalis's family to provide real time updates about what the news media was saying.

Whether the press realized it or not, their reports were also giving Khaalis real time information about operational moves the police were making or considering. These reports had dangerous consequences for those of us now captive. This became Khaalis's instant Internet access model way before the Internet became a way in life in America and the world.

In 2005, Raphael Cohen-Almagor from the University of Haifa in Israel wrote an article about media coverage during terrorist acts. Since the terrorist siege we were now living was an international media event, there were numerous references on what the media was doing and many of their actions were not helpful to us. The tone of his article entitled "Media Coverage of Acts of Terrorism: Troubling Episodes and Suggested Guidelines" in the *Canadian Journal of Communication, Vol 30, No 3* was one of astonishment to me. He wrote, for example, "When the police negotiators tried to build their credibility with the terrorists, one talk show journalist asked the Hanafi's: 'How can you believe the police?' It was as if an alliance had formed between the terrorists and the media against the police." Cohen-Almagor concluded media behavior during the siege put our lives in danger on more than one occasion.

While the terrorist siege was unfolding, the media were a part of the events and BJ was experiencing first hand the frenzy the media was creating. At one point, Khaalis became enraged when he heard a report that Max Robinson had done. He instructed BJ to call the station and get Robinson on the phone. She was told by the operator that Robinson was on the air and couldn't come to the phone. This made him angrier. BJ told the operator it was a matter of life and death and she needed to reach Robinson.

The operator finally gave her another number which would connect her to the producer in the control booth. She called and told them "Mr. Khaalis wanted to speak with Mr. Robinson." The producer spoke to Robinson in his ear piece about the call and Robinson got on. BJ handed Khaalis the phone. A friend of mine watching the news that night said that it looked like Robinson "turned white" as he picked up the phone and began the conversation. Khaalis told him that he wanted the station's General Manger to go on the air and retract the story.

My inclination was that did not happen. People were after a story and they obviously did not take into consideration people's lives were at stake. Those of us being held on the other side of the 8th floor had no idea that a new dimension of the siege had started late Wednesday afternoon.

The calls were not just from the local media. A Cliff Evans from WOR in New York City got through and he and Khaalis discussed the movie. Evans told Khaalis he was going to try and get Mustafa Akkad the producer of _Mohammad Messenger of God_ to call Khaalis. BJ gave him the numbers for all seven lines. Even if he reached Akkad, it was doubtful he would call Khaalis. Did Cliff Evans create some expectation for Khaalis that would never be fulfilled and what were the consequences for us?

Also on Wednesday, TV station WTTG in Washington showed a 40 second clip of the movie which Khaalis wanted stopped. It took viewers calling the station expressing concerns that the airing of the clip might actually endanger our lives to stop the airing. Other calls from the media that came in later in the siege proved to be even more problematic for us and the police as they worked through options.

One reporter, Jim Bohannon of WTOP Radio, got through and was so misinformed about who Khaalis was that he referred to Khaalis as a Black Muslim. This was the same group that killed his family in 1973. For this transgression, Khaalis told Bohannon that he was going to kill a hostage and throw him out the window. Perhaps it would have been one of my older colleagues who had been singled out as one of the first to die. If Bohannon had not gone on radio and TV to profusely apologize for the mistake, Khaalis might have carried out his threat. Thirty four years later I contacted Bohannon to check on the accuracy of the story. In an email exchange Bohannon told me "Boy do I remember that time! I anchored 21 straight hours on WTOP Radio from 10am the day it began till 7 am the next morning. Then, the next evening I went another 12 or 13 solo anchor hours till it finally ended. The article was close. Khaalis was monitoring WTOP and heard me early on describe the Hanafi's as "black muslims." This was as accurate as we could be at the time, and was technically true (they were black and they were muslim), but, of course the Hanafi's hated the major group principally known as Black Muslims. I'd stepped on a big cow plop, unwittingly. It was at this point that, unless I apologized on WTOP and (then co-owned) TV-9, Khaalis said he was going to "start cutting off heads at B'nai B'rith, putting them in paper bags, and dropping them out the window." Needless to say, I quickly did my apologizing, although I wasn't exactly dressed for tv."

Khaalis did discriminate in whom he would speak with. A *Washington Post* reporter got through Wednesday afternoon and when BJ told him who was on the phone, he told her he wouldn't speak with anyone from the *Post*. He was upset about the paper's coverage of him related to the killing of his family.

The terrorist siege that began on the morning of March 9, 1977, was happening in an era where there were neither cell phones nor internet or instant communications. Western Union still delivered telegrams. I'm not sure my daughters even know what a telegram was. There were no options to view hundreds of cable channels and have access to news 24 hours a day. Basically, every big city in America had three major TV channels, NBC, CBS and ABC. Perhaps there was an educational or local channel that few people viewed.

People received the bulk of their information from the three network channels and the newspapers in their communities. In an area like Washington, you were lucky to live in where you could pick up signals from Baltimore stations as well as the local Washington stations for some variety.

As the events unfolded in the B'nai B'rith Building, my colleagues and I had no notion that the event we were participants in would attract worldwide attention. I certainly knew what was transpiring in the B'nai B'rith Building since I was up close and personal. Life is about human interaction and there was a great deal of that occurring outside the building in the Washington area and thousands of miles away.

I was the only person from Miami, Florida, in the building and there were events in Miami that were occurring as well; they were personal and a bit complicated. I had had a falling out with my parents and older sister Eileen and older brother Michael over a rather silly family matter. The issue and the reaction it created from my parents, Eileen and Michael led me to sever ties with everyone in my family except for my brother Barry, who I had remained in contact with. I had not spoken with my parents, Eileen or Michael for nearly a year.

My brother-in-law Bobby (from Jane's side), who has been more like a brother to me for 40 years, was distraught over this turn of events. He would continually ask me if I had spoken with my family and would tell me how upset he was with me for not doing so. As news was starting to trickle out about what was happening in Washington, I had family members trying to figure out how to get reengaged with the outcast, namely me. I have to admit, the fact that I had not spoken to my family did not cross my mind while I was being held. Afterwards, it was an interesting perspective for me to dwell on as I learned what had happened in Miami between March 9-11, 1977.

For my parents, Eileen and Michael, the only conduit was Jane, and she started to receive calls from people she had not heard from for a year as well. To her credit, she was civil and took their calls. There were offers to come up to help out which she declined. Whether there were elements of guilt in the calls only Jane could read between the lines of their conversations.

As with most large cities, Miami had the three local station affiliates and two daily newspapers. The *Miami Herald*, the larger of the two papers published in the morning and the *Miami News* in the afternoon. I knew the *Miami News* well and intimately. My father George was a compositor for the *Miami News* in the 50's up until the late 60's. He set the type for the paper ever day. When I was growing up I'd visit the *News* building on Biscayne Boulevard. It was a grand old historic building that was a tower and interesting to me that the presses were located on upper floors. The printing area was dark and noisy. It was most fun to go on a Thursday and read the Sunday funnies that would appear with the paper a few days later.

Though my father was on the production side and not an executive with the paper, he had developed relationships with numerous people who were either reporters or involved in the editorial or business sides of managing the paper. He was well liked by his colleagues and I always thought his best contacts were with the sports writers and editors who were kind in providing tickets for Baltimore Orioles spring games which they played at Miami Stadium as well as Orange Bowl games. My dad's contacts allowed my friend David Fritsch and me to sit in a cold Orange Bowl and watch Joe Namath play his last collegiate game for Alabama against Texas.

One of my dad's friends was Howard Kleinberg, then managing editor of the paper who attended my Bar Mitzvah. By 1977, Kleinberg was the Managing Editor of the *Palm Beach Post*, the sister publication of the *Miami News*. When news of the siege was starting to get out by mid-day on March 9, the local TV stations were interrupting their broadcasts to provide what little information they had. My former sister-in-law Linda was pregnant with my nephew Steven and was home watching TV. She heard the B'nai

B'rith building mentioned and knew that was my office. She decided to call one of the stations and asked for the news room. Linda was upset and crying on the phone when someone answered her call. When they asked what was wrong, she told them she thought her brother-in-law was in the building mentioned. They asked for her name and address and she complied.

After that call she phoned my brother and reported what she had done. He told her he was on his way home and not to answer the door. I've never seen the interview, but I understand Linda had given an interview that afternoon and now the other stations and newspapers were in the hunt for information; they were trying to find out who I was and who might be related to me in Miami.

That afternoon my father called his friend Howard Kleinberg at the *Palm Beach Post*. He told Howard he was just hoping the newspapers might be receiving information on what was happening in Washington the general public might not be getting. At that point, no one knew much—not even if I was in the building. Howard told my father he wouldn't use the information in any way. My dad, quite naïve about these matters, believed him.

Kleinberg shared the information with people he knew at the *Miami News*. Since the *News* was now located in the same building as the bigger *Herald* to share production facilities for efficiencies, the *Herald* also got a heads-up about the information as well.

Beyond my father's call, the newspapers didn't have to do much investigative work. They just had to watch my sister-in-laws interview and the feeding frenzy was on. By late afternoon, when my wife Jane finally got home, she started to field calls from family. She had also been contacted by B'nai B'rith staff trying to confirm my whereabouts and the FBI requesting that families not speak with the press. She passed that information on to the family in Miami but I guess not everyone got the message.

That evening, my father gave an interview to the *Herald* that appeared the next morning. You would have thought that my family had spoken with me the day before the siege started.

On Thursday afternoon, the headline in the *Miami News* afternoon edition read—"UM GRADUATE HELD HOSTAGE IN DC"–and the article was written by Ian Glass. So much for Kleinberg's confidential conversation with his old friend George. It was an interesting article. The problem was that it just didn't contain much truth. Glass wrote that I was one of 57 hostages being held. He further indicated that the FBI had called Jane at home and told her that they had seen me through binoculars from a building across the street. I was sitting in a chair with my hands behind my back and there were another 14-15 people in the room with me. I only wish that was the truth. From his fingertips on his keyboard to God's ears would have been nice. In large measure, the article was totally fabricated.

Afterwards when I saw the article and the byline, I assumed the reporter was a young person and this was potentially a break for them in doing an article above the fold. That was a wrong assumption. As I learned, Ian Glass was a seasoned reporter for the *News* and had been associated with Howard Kleinberg for many years. Glass was a well respected reporter and editor. My father was quite upset with the article and called Kleinberg to tell him how he felt and that he hoped his actions had not jeopardized my life.

On that Wednesday, March 9th, my brother Barry was traveling back from Birmingham, Alabama, and did not know what was transpiring in Washington. His plane had a stop in Tallahassee, the state capital, and members of the state delegation from Miami were heading home.

Robert McKnight, a state senator, sat next to my brother and said it had been a bad day in the nation's capital. He gave him a brief synopsis and said he heard the B'nai B'rith Building mentioned. For the remainder of the trip until he landed in Miami and called his wife Diane, he had to wonder what exactly was going on. When he got home he had spoken with Jane and she filled him on what she knew and the restrictions not to speak with the press.

By that evening, he received a call from Robert Liss, a reporter from the *Miami Herald*. When Barry said they were not to speak with the press, Liss indicted that stories were appearing in the *Herald* the next morning from an interview my father gave and he told him of the interview on TV that Linda had given so there was no reason not to give an interview.

Barry decided to speak with him and try to clarify some issues that had been covered. My family had never interacted with the press—we had no reason to. They now were dealing with TV personalities and print media way more sophisticated than they were who were looking for the story. Jane's side of the family, who also lived in South Florida, was trying to figure out what was happening in Washington as well. My brother-in-law

Steven worked in the same stock brokerage office as my father-in-law Sidney. Sidney was suffering from severely formed cataracts on both eyes and had trouble reading the newspaper and seeing the stock quote screen on his desk. Someone came over to my brother-in-law's cube and said he had just seen something come across the news wire about a hostage incident in Washington and the B'nai B'rith Building was mentioned.

Steven had my private number, he dialed it and got no answer. He tried a number of times and received the same response. He decided not to share with Sidney until he had more information. Later that afternoon Steven told him something was happening in Washington and there was a good chance that I might be involved.

The two sides of the family were always cordial with one another when they got together though Jane's side, watching the news stories coming from my side of the family, became disconcerted. The two sides of the family were calling each other discussing who would go to Washington as representatives of the family. They were stymied by Jane's insistence that no one come. On Wednesday afternoon Jane heard from Vicki Franklin an old friend from New Jersey who offered to come to Washington to help out and be with her. This offer of assistance she accepted. In Miami, the two families had also decided on a course of action and were planning to make travel arrangements. If things went bad and if I was killed, my brother Barry and my father-in-law Sidney were going to be on their way.

While Khaalis was speaking with the press, his men continued to monitor what was happening outside the building and to deal with their hostages. As Wednesday wore on from 2:00 pm until dark, the work crews continued their mission of taking apart B'nai B'rith's internal office structure and stopping up the stairwells.

Late Wednesday afternoon one our colleagues, Bernice, became hysterical. Her reaction was understandable since the stress and tension had not abated. Latif told the women sitting near Bernice to calm her down. He wanted everyone to remain as serene as possible. There was no question the terrorists did not want to deal with a lot of disruptive people.

CHAPTER EIGHTEEN

ZAHEDI AND MULLANY CONVERGE

By Wednesday afternoon, Ambassador Zahedi had arrived at Dulles Airport on an Air France Concorde flight. He was met by State Department and police officials who escorted him to the Iranian Embassy where he would meet up with his ambassador counterparts from Egypt and Pakistan. Though well known and popular, he had never experienced a full police escort with sirens blaring and clearing traffic.

Ambassador Zahedi knew Washington and the United States well. He had received his undergraduate degree in agricultural engineering from Utah State University in the early 1950's. He also experienced other aspects of America as a young man working in a steel mill in the Chicago area and washing dishes in New Orleans.

As the escort came into the District of Columbia, one of his first impressions was a feeling the capital of America was under siege. Police were everywhere. Numerous streets had been barricaded and the sound of helicopters in the skies was constant.

Within a short time of being back in Washington, Ambassador Zahedi had conversations with a number of U.S. Senators who were close personal friends who visited with him at the Embassy. Senator Jacob Javits of New York and Charles Percy of Illinois encouraged him to help. He also heard from his friend Howard Baker the senator from Tennessee.

After his arrival a number of aides briefed him on what they knew from the police and State Department. A council member, Marion Barry, had been shot and a young reporter had been killed. He also learned that the leader of the terrorists was identified as a Hanafi Muslim. The Ambassador knew the Hanafi sect had extreme fundamentalist views about how the Islamic religion should be adhered. A Shia himself, the Ambassador was concerned how Khaalis might react to him.

After further discussions among the three ambassadors, they decided to go to the police command center and become actively involved in trying to save lives. In addition, Ambassador Zahedi was concerned about his own family, his daughter and former wife. He didn't know the scope and range of who was involved from the Hanafi movement and didn't want his participation to put his family in danger. Part of the agreement the ambassadors had with the police was that their involvement be secret and inconspicuous. The ambassadors wanted no press notification that they were involved.

When Patrick Mullany arrived in Washington after the short flight from Cleveland, he sensed the turmoil in the city and had a similar reaction to Ambassador Zahedi's. The only information he had was very scant as he got off the plane. He knew there had been an incident at the District Building and that's where he decided to head.

He jumped into a cab and asked the driver to take him to the District Building. The driver looked at him like he was crazy and asked if he knew what was going on? He refused to take him. Mullany pulled his FBI credentials, showed them to the driver and he finally agreed to take him.

As they crossed over the 14th Street bridge, they could see red lights rotating and sirens going. The driver also briefed him about other buildings that had been attacked. He mentioned the Islamic Center and the B'nai B'rith Building over on Rhode Island Avenue. He said the "whole damn town was under siege." As they approached Constitution Avenue and 12th Street, they were stopped by a police barricade. Mullany again produced his credentials and they let the cab through. Arriving at the corner near the District Building, both of them noticed a body lying on the sidewalk that was covered by a sheet. Mullany got out of the cab and the driver sped off. The driver was way closer to what was happening in Washington then he ever wanted.

As Mullany walked towards the front door of the District Building, he couldn't help but glance again at the body covered by the sheet. At the time, he didn't know he was looking at Maurice Williams, the young reporter who had been slain by a shotgun blast in the initial stages of the siege. He next noticed City Council member Marion Barry standing by the door with a deep red stain in the center of his chest from a gunshot wound near his heart. Police and emergency personnel were everywhere. Patrick Mullany knew he was in America but felt he had entered a war zone. The sketchy information he received in Cleveland didn't approximate what he was witnessing and experiencing. The city of Washington was truly under siege.

He decided to enter the District Building. By that time, the shooting had stopped and it was strangely quiet. He walked up the staircase to a halfway point where a large desk had been placed across the opening of the stairs. It served as a barricade and obstruction from further gun fire. Police tactical squads were in place at different points on the floor. He moved around the desk quietly walking up the remaining stairs to the top floor. He could see the office where the terrorists had placed furniture at the front as a barricade. The corridor outside the office was wide and open. No one could have made their way across the opening without being seen by the terrorists. Sixty feet away, out in the open, he saw an individual lying prone and still. He at first thought the person had been killed. Later he learned it was a person caught in the open when the siege began who decided to remain in that position and play dead. Mullany made his way back down the stairs. It was time to locate the police command center.

CHAPTER NINETEEN

INTERESTING THINGS DEVELOPING ON THE 8ᵀᴴ FLOOR

As Wednesday wore on and the women and men were separated on opposite sides of the room, we were able to look across at one another. They were faces of fear and a lack of comprehension as to what had happened to us–quizzical looks about what might happen at any moment. Though we couldn't speak, we could communicate with our eyes, facial expressions and nodding of heads. Nothing more than that simple act was needed. There were also looks of empathy and support as colleagues sought out their friends and close acquaintances. People were able to give strength to one another even across the room. The women looked across at the men with a great deal of sympathy seeing the discomfort they were beginning to display from having their hands tied behind their backs as well as a variety of visible injuries.

There was also an interesting phenomenon developing on the 8ᵗʰ floor that had the potential to damage reputations and relationships among colleagues. This hostage event had created a new and different social stratum that none of us were used to or had experienced before as B'nai B'rith employees. It didn't matter what your title or job was; it didn't matter how much money you made or how much your clothes cost; nor did it matter if in your own mind you thought you were smarter or better than the individuals you worked with. Everyone up on the 8ᵗʰ floor was equal. The young men who worked in the mail room were just as equal as senior executives of the organization. As all the men were tied up and the windows were being darkened, the terrorist's continued their threats of death.

95

A senior executive pleaded with the terrorist to talk with Khaalis to work things out. He was told to be quiet but persisted in his pleading. This only enraged the terrorists further and they told everyone that if we didn't remain quiet people would be killed.

Another senior executive also refused to remain quiet and was taking a posture that, "don't they know who I am" and "how could they be doing this to me." They obviously didn't care that this person had such a high regard for himself–if he didn't be quiet they would kill him and others. I watched in amusement as a young man who worked in the mailroom turned to this senior executive and told him to shut up.

What I was observing was that people who thought they could turn to those with senior positions for strength were disappointed in how they were handling the situation. In fairness to all my colleagues being held and labeled a hostage, no one had training or life experiences to prepare them physically and emotionally for being a hostage. I know it wasn't on my resume. However, I think one begins to call upon one's intuitive nature to figure out what one should or should not do to maximize your survival odds. It was amazing and scary to watch people let their inflated egos over-take them and get in the way. Not only were endangering themselves, but others as well. Their actions were being noted by all their colleagues and resentment towards them was building.

As I looked down the line of men, two truly worried me. Joe Sklover, the Chief Financial Officer, had suffered a heart attack some time ago. Hank Siegel, from the Public Relations Department, also had a bad heart condition.

Hank's ordeal was a recent memory since it was a very public event. During the 1976 Convention in Washington, Hank suffered a severe heart attack in his room late one night. Steve Morrison, who had operational responsibilities in managing the overall convention, received a call from the hotel staff alerting him about the problems Hank was experiencing. Hank, at some point during his heart attack, was able to call the hotel operator and ask for help. An emergency medical team from the District of Columbia took him to the hospital. Hank's condition was serious and he almost died. At the start of the general session the next morning, attendees were asked to stand and say a silent prayer for Hank's recovery. He did survive and while excellent medical attention was paramount, the power of prayer most likely didn't hurt.

CHAPTER TWENTY

THE NEGOTIATING TEAM FORMS

Late Wednesday afternoon, the three ambassadors were finally together with the police. When Ambassador Zahedi arrived at the command center he thought the atmosphere chaotic. No one knew what was happening in the buildings; they didn't have a handle on how many terrorists were involved; and they didn't have a clue as to how many hostages there were, particularly in the B'nai B'rith building with hundreds of employees.

B'nai B'rith couldn't accurately figure out which employees were in the office at 11:00am on March 9th. They sure didn't know about non-employee's who might have been caught up in the siege. The police did know they were dealing with Hamas Abdul Khaalis, knew his history and were concerned about how to manage what was happening in the city.

In the command center, Mullany was trying to grasp the full extent of what was occurring. From his experience, the most important phase of negotiations was to ascertain why an individual, or in our case a group of individuals, used violence. His initial gut check told him this situation was way different than any he had ever encountered. Observing the body on the street by the District Building and knowing shots had been fired at other locations significantly altered what they were facing. As he and his colleagues were developing their hostage negotiation expertise, they realized when a life was lost the difficulty of conducting a negotiation became very different. He knew in his heart that he was involved in the worst terrorism and hostage negotiation law enforcement authorities ever faced. When the District of Columbia police and federal officials gathered at the Police

Command Center, it was unclear whether the three buildings were connected or if they were facing three separate incidents? From his perspective and after listening to tapes the police made of their initial discussions with Khaalis, Mullany knew the events were indeed connected. FBI Director Clarence Kelley came to the Command Center to be briefed by Mullany. One of his first questions was whether Mullany thought the buildings were connected. Mullany took Kelley through the tapes he had just listened to and reviewed the facts why the three buildings were connected.

Mullany also heard Khaalis's voice live for the first time. As I had heard on the 2nd floor landing with my colleagues, Mullany listened to Khaalis's demands. He said the killers of his family never received justice. He told Deputy Chief Rabe, "The Koran teaches us an eye for an eye and a tooth for a tooth." He was adamant the killers of his family be brought to him so he could administer justice. Khaalis told Rabe that "You house and feed them-that is not justice." He further added, "Bring them to me and I will do what Allah would command us to do." He would behead these men. Mullany was convinced that Khaalis would do exactly that if he had the ability to do so.

The leadership of the Command Center was starting to form. At the command center were Police Chief Maurice Cullinane, Deputy Chief Rabe, who had the initial conversation with Khaalis, Joseph O'Brien who was involved in the investigation of Khaalis's family and Khaalis trusted him and Patrick Mullany's colleague Nick Stames who was the Special Agent in Charge of the Washington office. Mullany knew Bob Rabe well having worked with him on the State Department's Committee to Combat Terrorism that Ambassador Meyer had initiated. He highly respected Rabe's abilities and his street smarts. In the beginning stages, due to his relationship with Khaalis, O'Brien would conduct the discussions.

As the severity of the task began to unfold, Mullany realized psychological profiling would be incredibly difficult. When Khaalis was a young man and served in the military he had been diagnosed with a mental illness. Mullany's initial analysis determined this was not part of the equation they were dealing with. They were more concerned about Khaalis's deep religious convictions and how these convictions meshed with the horrific killings of his family. Mullany knew they were dealing with an individual who had swayed 11 of his followers to take up his cause even though innocent lives might be taken. With a more complete picture emerging about the challenge ahead, Mullany went to Police Chief Cullinane and recommended they contact two psychiatrists that he worked with to provide assistance–Robert Blum and Steve Pieczenik. Blum was in private practice and Pieczenik was a Deputy Assistant Secretary of State who worked with the Department's Terrorism Committee. Mullany felt they would be particularly helpful in evaluating Khaalis's medical records. Also joining the group from time to time was Earl J. Silbert, who was the District of Columbia's United States Attorney. When Khaalis demanded the killers of his family brought to him, Silbert was the liaison with the Director of Prisons in finding out where they were being held.

The format developed in speaking with Khaalis was relatively simple. It was decided that Rabe would replace O'Brien as the voice of the police authorities on a speaker phone. Also sitting around the table were Mullany, Blum and Pieczenik. Each man had a legal pad and would scribble notes to Rabe asking Khaalis to clarify a statement or raise an important point. Khaalis didn't realize he was actually talking to more than one person. Mullany had the ability to listen to Khaalis's voice and his concern about reaching a successful conclusion was rising. He kept thinking how different this hostage siege was. He knew they were dealing with, as Mullany would describe him, "a rigid, forceful, intelligent person who had the charisma to have 11 followers willing to carry out his every wish even if it meant killing innocent people. He was a respected religious leader with a strong following that had been deeply offended by the killing of his family. His motivation was to deliver justice as the Koran and Allah commanded him to do—to behead the killers."

Later that afternoon, after meeting at the Iranian Embassy, the three ambassadors came to the Command Center to be briefed. They listened to tapes of the initial conversations with Khaalis. Much of what they heard was highly anti-Semitic. As Mullany looked at the ambassadors he saw what they were listening to made them uneasy. The irony was not lost on Mullany–they were asking three Arab ambassadors to negotiate basically for Jewish lives though people of many faiths were being held. He also saw in each of the men an acknowledgement of the situation and that their help was indeed needed. Mullany also thought of another irony of fate–the connection between Khaalis and Abdul Jabbar and a connection Mullany had to Jabbar. He first met the then Lew Alcindor when he was in the 7th grade at St. Elizabeth's School on the Upper West Side of New York. Mullany was coaching a basketball team at Good Shepherd School and he remembered Alcindor as a clumsy and awkward boy, growing by leaps and bounds who had trouble dribbling the basketball. He had his team double team him throughout the game and they won. The loss to Mullany's team didn't dim Lew Alcindor's talents and aspirations for the future. It was simply the irony of the connection Mullany couldn't displace from his mind.

As the evening hours approached the noise of a city under siege remained ringing in our ears. There didn't seem to be a minute that would go by when you did not hear a police siren. Where they were going and what they were doing was unknown. Occasionally we would hear the thump of helicopter blades. Sometimes it seemed they were close enough to the B'nai B'rith Building that if you had the ability to walk over to a window and look out, you would be able to see the pilot's face. At other times the sound was distant.

As it became darker, the work being done by the young men on the B'nai B'rith staff began to subside. When they came back into the room, those who had been forced to serve on work crews looked exhausted. The trauma of the hostage siege and the physical exertion of clogging up the stairwells had taken a toll on them.

I wondered, was it a welcome relief when they were done and retied up? It was painful having your arms extended all the way up your back and your hands tied together and all of them were being retied. It also occurred to me those who served on the work crews probably realized true physical danger in being with the terrorists in such close proximity under very trying conditions. What if they were not performing their tasks as well as the terrorists wanted? We had witnessed numerous times since 11:00 am that even the slightest circumstance could upset the terrorists and cause them to become agitated. While our colleagues worked, the risk to be injured or killed increased greatly.

Ever since the opening segments of the siege at 11:00 am, the police were looking at the building from different vantage points and monitoring people looking out of office windows. They could see that a number had not been taken hostage and were either barricaded in offices, as Lawrie Kaplan had done to save colleagues from capture, or hiding from the terrorists.

The question was when could they develop an action plan to extract people from the building not being held on the 8th floor. The police must have started to probe the building later that night and discovered the debris pile that had been created in each of the stairwells. They would need to proceed cautiously. They didn't know if the terrorists were on other floors. They also didn't know who the people were in the offices they identified for rescue.

CHAPTER TWENTY ONE

ALL ALONE

Errol Imber, who worked within the Jewish Adult Education area, was in his office at the far end of the 5th floor where my office was located. Errol's was the last office on the floor and if you didn't walk all the way down the hall you might not have noticed it. We happened to do two opposite things that day. I walked down the stairwell to investigate the noise coming from the lower part of the building. Errol looked down the hall from his office, wasn't sure what the commotion was, and went back into his office and closed his door and sat down. As noise on the 5th floor became louder, Errol opened his door slightly and glanced down the hall way. He heard shouting and instructions for people not to move or they would be killed. He quietly closed his door, locked it and sat back at his desk.

He considered using the phone but realized the line light would also light up at a desk outside his office and he didn't want that light to cause any interest in his location. Every so often he would look out the window and cautiously glance around but mostly he sat at his desk, looking at the door, trying to remain as quiet as possible.

Sometime Wednesday afternoon, though he didn't realize it, he was spotted by the police and they had an idea where he was located. Later he heard noise near his office. He didn't know it but the work crews had arrived to grab furniture and other items to clog up the stairwells. If someone held a mirror to Errol's mouth, it would have been hard to ascertain if he was actually breathing. He was working on controlling his emotions and his fright. He noticed that someone was trying his door knob and he truly stopped breathing. They gave it a few tries and whoever was on the other side, finally gave up. He never knew if it was one of the terrorists or a colleague on the work crews. He had quickly determined that he was not going to open the door and find out.

As it became dark on Wednesday, the police decided to make some forays into the building and see what they encountered. Throughout the afternoon, they had spotted people in offices such as Errol and they wanted to try and rescue them from the building if at all possible. Cautiously and carefully they tried, floor-by-floor. They wanted to get to the 5th floor as they knew that a number of people were there.

They found the stairwells jammed with debris and needed to proceed carefully. They didn't know if the terrorists had rigged any explosives. As the police made their plans sizing up the challenge, Errol sat at his desk, in the dark, waiting. Waiting for what, he wasn't sure. He still did not want to use the phone concerned the line light might alert someone where he was. For all he knew, people were just outside his door and he had heard threats of death being shouted when the siege began. Later in the evening, someone wasn't just trying the door knob, for there was a loud knock and someone telling him to open the door. He sat there and said nothing.

The police, as they rescued colleagues from offices, were being just as guarded. They didn't know how many terrorists they were dealing with and were not sure who exactly was behind the closed doors.

The person on the other side of Errol's door told him they knew he was in there and they were the police. Errol finally found his voice and told them he didn't know if they were the police and they needed to prove it.

I'm not sure under those circumstances I would have had all my mental faculties working properly to make such a reasonable request. The police officer on the other side of the door, a member of the DC SWAT team, told Errol he would slide his identification under the door and then gave him some very specific instructions. This scene was being repeated in other parts of the building where colleagues had holed up since the siege began. Once Errol saw the identification and could see they were the police, he was to unlock the door and then laid face down on the floor and not move a muscle. By the tone in his voice, Errol knew the person giving the orders was serious. Errol looked at the identification, unlocked the door and quickly lied face down on his office floor. The door was opened and there were a number of people in his office some kneeling next to him and he could feel their weapons against him. They expertly checked him for any weapons and then helped him to his feet. It was dark out and dark in Errol's office and he was trying to adjust his sight. Now, he was looking face-to- face with a few men who were big, wearing dark outfits and each one had a large rifle. Additionally, the men in his office had blond hair and blue eyes. Though they told him they were the police and he saw some identification he still wasn't sure they were really police. For a moment in time, Errol's eyes were telling his brain that the B'nai B'rith Building had been taken over by the American Nazi Party and these men were part of that effort.

One might think Errol's reaction was a strong bias or paranoia but in reality was not that farfetched from a personal experience. In the summer of 1975, I made a trip to the District 2 Convention in St. Louis, Missouri to handle a Young Leadership session and interact with volunteer leaders. The district encompassed parts of the Midwest and Rocky Mountain states. The meeting was being held at the Chase Park Plaza a famous stately hotel in downtown St. Louis. After flying in from Miami, where I had left Jane and Emily to stay with her parents, I took an airport van to the hotel. As I got off the van, directly across the street were a number of young men dressed in full Nazi regalia who were picketing the District 2 meeting holding signs that had vile messages about the Jewish people. I had never experienced such a spectacle before. They seemed menacing and were hoping for reaction from convention attendees that would allow them to react in kind. Based on my own experience, Errol's thoughts, at least to me under the circumstances were very logical.

CHAPTER TWENTY TWO

DAY BECOMES NIGHT

As night fell, the terrorists were settling into a routine. They kept two guards on the hostages sitting in chairs on either end of the room with rifles across their laps and their terrorist compatriots guarding the stairwells. Khaalis was in his command center with BJ placing and answering calls.

For the first and only time, they read to us from a publication describing the inadequacies and errors that they felt were in the movie *Mohammed Messenger of God*. Abdul Salaam did the honors. He read in a monotone and showed little passion. I surmised that he was ordered to do so by Khaalis and he read to us for about 20 minutes. Perhaps they wanted us to know that these injustices justified what they were doing. None of my colleagues were paying much attention to Salaam's reading. We tried to seem attentive and I guess that gesture satisfied him. If he was going to test us afterwards, most likely many of us would have failed. The sympathies I was feeling certainly were not focused on our captors but on my colleagues who were suffering at the injustices being heaped on us.

Most of the incoming calls BJ was answering were coming from reporters. This tied up the lines and it became difficult for police to contact Khaalis when they wanted to speak with him. BJ didn't know at the time that some of the calls that she would handle later that evening would be the ambassadors' first attempt to speak with Khaalis to try and reason with him and develop some rapport. The police were also working to tap all the active lines coming into B'nai B'rith in addition to phone lines at the

District Building and Islamic Center. Later that night they had succeeded in activating the wire taps which gave them more information.

The issue of reporters agitating the terrorists wasn't limited to the B'nai B'rith Building. Cohen-Almagor wrote that at the District Building the terrorists who had killed Maurice Williams, wounded Marion Barry and Mack Cantrell and paralyzed one of the hostages, Robert Pierce, with a shotgun blast, were monitoring radio broadcasts as well. One of the hostages was Alan Grip, an aide to Councilman Sterling Tucker. Grip heard the broadcast that reported a fire ladder being setup outside the District Building with police climbing up the ladder. The reporter implied the police were going to break into the building. Grip said "one of the gunmen went crazy." He screamed, "You tell the police to take that ladder away or we're gonna start blowing people away." It looked like Alan Grip's day was reflective of mine. We were a short distance from one another, in very similar situations and just didn't know it at the time.

It was now completely dark outside on March 9th. We also had some luck regarding the weather. March could be cold in Washington and we were experiencing some milder days. If it had been colder, our situation would have been much more uncomfortable. Even so, the hard floor was colder than being on a carpeted area. The terrorists had located newspapers and cardboard and started to place them on the floor where the women were gathered along the window line facing out to Rhode Island Avenue. I'm sure for the women, it provided some relief to the hard floor and cold that they felt. Many of them were wearing dresses or skirts and were able to use the newspapers to cover up their legs.

For the men, there was no such relief. I was guessing that it was about 10:00 pm, and it had been close to 11 hours that our hands hand been tied behind our backs. I stopped hearing jet planes and knew that National Airport stopped accepting traffic at that time so that was probably a good guess. The terrorists wanted us to be quiet and settled. It was obviously going to be a long night. We were told to be absolutely quiet and not talk but we would continually violate that order by whispering to one another. From the beginning of the siege it was obvious that a defense mechanism was to make yourself as inconspicuous as possible–don't attract attention to yourself and agitate the terrorists. In my mind, that was a goal to work towards. They tried to adjust the lighting in the room so it would be dark over the women and remain bright over the men. They were highly unsuccessful at their attempts and gave up after 15 minutes and kept the lights on the 8th floor. As in counting the number of hostages at the outset, light adjusting could be added to the skill sets they needed work on.

CHAPTER TWENTY THREE

COLLEAGUES

I finally had stopped my face from bleeding late Wednesday afternoon and could feel that it was crusted with blood. It was quite swollen and I could tell the difference when I would lie with the left side of my face on the floor compared to the side where I took the hit from the rifle barrel. Though it hurt, it really wasn't comparable to the pain that was creeping up in my shoulders. As I looked at my colleagues, no one was complaining about their pain and I couldn't help but wonder, am I the only one feeling that my shoulders were exploding and were separating? In the end, without speaking with one another, it was almost as if a collective decision had been made to suffer in silence. On the men's side of the room, two rows had been formed naturally. One was close to the wall and those positioned there had an ability to place their backs against the wall which provided some comfort. The other row, which I was in, was in front of this group; basically we were lying on the floor. I have to admit, as Wednesday evening wore on, I was jealous of my colleagues who were in the back row. They seemed a bit more comfortable then the group lying in the front row. Soon though, they noticed our difficulty of lying on the floor without any support. Those against the wall offered up their legs for the person in front to lean on which took some pressure off your back. Jay Manchester was right behind me. He put his legs up and I was able to lean against them. Some were using other people's shoes to get their heads off the floor. My wallet had fallen out of my pants and people were pushing it with their noses to use it as a pillow. During most of the evening I was lying next to Dale

Bell who was the Director of Human Resources at B'nai B'rith. Dale asked me "Are you through with that wallet?" and I said "Yes" He asked, "Can you push that thing over with your head towards me?" After I pushed it towards him, he pushed it along with his nose and grabbed it with his teeth so he could position it to use a pillow– a very small pillow.

Dale, who was not Jewish, was a soft spoken, nice man with three or four young children. As I looked at him, I was wondering if he was thinking that he'd never see his wife and children again. At times, I could surmise that was what colleagues must have been pondering for they looked sad–it was in their eyes and faces.

Later that evening Dale and I were still next to each other, not whispering, just both lost in our own thoughts. Then, out of the blue, Dale quietly said to me, "I'm going to tell them I'm Jewish. I asked Dale, "What are you talking about?" He looked over at me and once again said he'd tell them he's Jewish. He added that if the terrorists started asking people if they were Jewish to be killed, he was going to tell them yes he was Jewish. He continued to look at me and said, under the circumstances we were in, he Dale Bell, was just as Jewish as I was.

For the remainder of my life, I will never forget that conversation. To me, this statement was Dale's act of courage and bravery. If the terrorists had done such a thing, no one, including Dale's wife and children would have known of Dale's act of courage. There was no doubt in my mind he would have done what he said. Now, people will know.

Bernie Simon was also lying next to me. Though he had been untied as one of the older men, he was still uncomfortable. Bernie was a fairly big man and he offered me his hip to place my head on if that would be helpful. I declined but was touched and grateful for his generosity and kindness. Once I heard Bernie talking to himself and saying it will be a mess, it will all be wiped out. I asked him what he was talking about. He said the pension fund. Though Bernie was head of Public Relations, employees would joke that he spent more time as the administrator of the pension plan than PR. Many were happy that he was protecting our interests on very personal financial matters. He was almost like a groaning broken record. He kept repeating, "It will all be wiped out" and he couldn't believe it. Bernie was looking around the room at all the people being held captive, the vast majority of whom were in the pension plan.

He was doing calculations in his head. His last word on it to me was there would be nothing left.

Bernie would never have known it, but by Thursday afternoon Jane was near a number of wives who were discussing the pension plan. Many of them were older than Jane and had mortgage payments and college and weddings to pay for. They were relieved that if anything happened there was life insurance and the pension plan. I wonder how they would have felt about Bernie's calculations.

As the minutes and hours went by, Bernie and I quietly had a conversation on whether a number of us or all of us might be taking a trip to a faraway place if the terrorists were offered a large plane and a big sum of money. In actuality, that conversation did take place between the police and Khaalis. At one point they wanted to know if he wanted passage to another country, with the assumption being an Islamic nation. Khaalis's response was why would he want that. He was American and he had no intention of going anywhere. So much for the plane ride.

At another point Wednesday night, I was lying next to Jerry Rudman. I knew Jerry as an associate and we'd both probably say that we were not friends. We had never socialized and our families did not know one another. We had no idea that our wives, Jane and Paula, were being introduced to one another under less than optimal circumstances and were developing a relationship based on a personal bonding that few get or want a chance to experience.

Jane had taken Jerry's youngest daughter with her when she picked up Emily at day care late Wednesday afternoon. Jerry and Paula's townhouse was not far from our apartment in Silver Spring. From that point Jane and Paula were in constant contact for the next 40 hours exchanging information and giving each other support as best they could. Jerry and I were injured hostages together and were learning about each other's sense of humor and compassion. First, we asked each other how the other was feeling. Since Jerry was the controller of the organization, I asked him how much cash we had downstairs in the accounting department. I said maybe Khaalis would like some money to go away. Jerry said that we didn't have much cash on hand, but he had the organization's checkbook and could always write out a check to him no matter what the amount. We looked at each other and smiled and both agreed that maybe we should just ask him how much he'd like the check to be. We also joked that since they had seven people we could lend them two of our staff to make it nine against nine in a softball game and if we won, he'd let us go free. It was probably better that we never tested Khaalis sense of humor about the money and softball game.

CHAPTER TWENTY FOUR

NOTHING THEY HAVE FACED BEFORE

In the Police Command Center, the day was becoming long and arduous. Later Wednesday, the ambassadors were sitting at the table with the group that had started to conduct negotiations with Khaalis. It was agreed the ambassadors would use passages from the Koran. After the briefing at the command center had been completed, the ambassadors would use a strategy of incorporating themes from the Koran that focused on compassion, forgiveness and understanding. Ambassador Ghorbal also placed a call to his political counselor for advice on passages and was provided with various quotes to use. Ambassador Zahedi called Mohammas Javad Farzaneh a Middle Eastern scholar, who lived in Bethesda, Maryland for guidance.

Ambassador Yaqub-Kahn was the first to reach out to Khaalis on the phone. The feeling was that Khaalis's ego would be fulfilled if people of such statue were speaking with him and the sound of Khaalis's voice seemed to confirm that. However, they were quickly reminded how volatile a person they were dealing with. At first Khaalis was honored and a bit embarrassed. He indicated that he did not trust the person to whom he was speaking. He also felt that he was being preached to. Khaalis became short with Ambassador Kahn and said to him, "Don't try to teach me, I know the Koran better then you do."

Sometime later, Ambassador Zahedi had his first opportunity to speak with Khaalis. Though he was briefed about Khaalis, the ambassador did not even know his name. All he knew was the person was very angry and that he was threatening to kill hostages.

115

Ambassador Zahedi always felt that when you entered negotiations in any kind of situation, it was imperative to know from both sides the circumstances that caused the disagreement. In his initial conversations he felt he was truly at a disadvantage since he did not know the full extent of the grievances that caused this man to attack buildings, kill and hurt people and take hostages.

During one of their initial discussions Khaalis spoke at length about the murder of his family. He gave Ambassador Zahedi a lesson on the Black Muslim movement. The ambassador had heard of Malcolm X but was not that familiar with the group and surrounding issues. He repeated all of his demands to the ambassador. He spoke about the movie *Mohammed Messenger of God* and its blasphemous nature. Sometime later, Ambassador Zahedi spoke with his King and mentioned the movie. The ambassador had not seen the movie but the Shah had. The ambassador told the Shah about this particular grievance and the Shah told the ambassador that he didn't think what the movie depicted would cause anyone to be upset.

As the ambassador listened to Khaalis's story and demands, he felt sad about Khaalis's family. He also felt that perhaps this was a basis to find a way to end the siege and to work with this man as he had done hundreds of times with people from around the world. He understood at least a part of Khaalis's motivation.

Even to the ambassador, Khaalis continued to reiterate his demands—he wanted the killers of his family brought to him. As the ambassador listened, he was careful to tell Khaalis that as an ambassador, he had no official standing with the police or government and could not deliver on any of his demands. The ambassador tried to convey thoughts and feelings to Khaalis that it would be best to end the hostage siege peacefully. Throughout Wednesday evening the ambassador made little progress in ending the crisis.

CHAPTER TWENTY FIVE

THE WILD SWINGS OF
A HOSTAGE'S FATE

Even though the men were tied, just to keep us off guard the terrorists would move us around. Unfortunately, at least though Wednesday evening, I was never rotated to the back wall. As I looked around at the men, it occurred to me that I was seeing people that I didn't know. Perhaps they had come into the building that morning or they actually worked for B'nai B'rith and I never met them. I was trying to figure out who they were and wondered if they had similar thoughts. I felt sad that I did not know them and pledged to myself when this was over, I'd make an effort to get to know these people.

I saw Hank Siegel and he appeared very drawn; I thought he was going to have a heart attack and die on us right there. The terrorists found a board for Hank to lie on rather than the hard floor and tried to make him more comfortable. They also retied his hands from the back to the front. Joe Sklover, who also had suffered a previous heart attack, asked the terrorists if he could also get a board to lie on. Since Joe was labeled one of the older gentlemen, his hands were untied and his was allowed to find a board. I looked on in awe as Joe showed a burst of energy to locate a good sized board. He carried it back to the middle of floor to lie on as well. I was impressed by Joe and if I had the capacity to clap, I would have applauded.

Even after Hank was lying on the board he still looked very ill and his breathing seemed to be labored. Marilyn Bargteil and I were looking across at each other and she nodded her head towards Hank. I nodded back and looked down at Hank. We communicated with our eyes that we were concerned about him and frankly, we thought he might die.

Sometime later Latif, who had been in and out of the room a number of times, noticed Hank lying in the middle of the floor. Latif and Khaalis, standing near the opening to the room, were having a conversation and looking over at Hank. Khaalis had his men untie Hank's hands. I guess they finally realized that a small man with a bad heart would not be a threat to them. Hank remained in that state throughout the night. Those of us who knew Hank were praying and hopeful that he was not going to die in the middle of the room.

As the night wore on, BJ continued to handle calls for Khaalis though they had subsided from the frenzy of Wednesday afternoon. A number of calls late Wednesday evening were coming from overseas, one from a reporter in Australia.

Khaalis continued to speak with his family during the night calling them every hour and also periodically checked in with his men at the District Building and the Islamic Center. He always reminded them to be on alert and stay calm. After Khaalis found BJ to help him work the phone system, he wanted her to call her mother and let her know she was ok. It was about 6:30 pm on Wednesday. In addition, to show his gratitude for her help, he said he would not kill her when the shooting started and told her to hide under the desk near the phones. She told Khaalis that she'd rather call her boyfriend Ira. He made her write the number down so he'd know what number she was calling. There was no answer. She wondered what Khaalis would think if he knew that Ira worked for *The New York Times* and if he'd be displeased with her. After another late night call, Khaalis looked at BJ and wondered whether anyone slept out there. With the phone quieter as Wednesday turned into Thursday BJ tried Ira again at 12:30 am Thursday. This time Ira answered and she told him she was ok and to please let her mother and the rest of the family know. In spite of Khaalis telling her that he would not kill her, BJ still had major doubts whether she would see Ira and her family again. She was privy to most of Khaalis's conversations where he continued to indicate to all he spoke with that he would kill the hostages if his demands were ignored.

The terrorists never let their guard down. You could see they were tense and concerned about the police attacking the building to free us. Either very late Wednesday evening or very early Thursday morning we heard a gunshot by the far stairwell. It was loud and got our attention quickly. Next we heard Khaalis yelling down the stairwell that the police better back off and not come any closer or they would be met by gunfire and he would start executing people and throw their heads down the stairwell. I'm not sure if Khaalis heard the police clearing people off the 5th floor or that the police were trying to make their way up the stairwell to see what the reaction might be. If that was part of the police plan, they certainly found out.

During the night the terrorists rotated among themselves, sitting in chairs watching us and being on the other part of the 8th floor. In addition to watching the elevators and stairwells they were taking turns to rest. It had been over 12 hours since they had captured the building. Although operating on adrenaline, they had to be tired after the physical and emotional exertion that was required. They had to remain vigilant as well.

Something interesting happened on the 8th floor in the very early hours of Thursday morning. On the other side of the floor from where we were being held, there was a room that was still under construction. You could see the door way from where we were situated. Without any warning, a loud gunshot went off and a plume of dust came out of the room.

My first inclination was that the police had infiltrated the building and the shooting had started. The tension level among us hostages rose quickly. As the gunshot occurred, I was able to observe a few things that I found interesting and actually somewhat comforting. The two terrorists who were in the chairs watching us both fell to the ground. A terrorist who was near the elevator also fell to the ground. All three of them looked scared and they didn't react very well to what might have been a potential crisis for them. The only terrorist who didn't hesitate in any fashion was Khaalis. I saw him immediately head to the room and go in. He seemed fearless. It took a moment before he reappeared along with another terrorist. I saw all the terrorists speak among themselves and then they all started to laugh. The terrorists were using the room as a rest area. One of them had lied down to catch some sleep and did so with a .357 Magnum on his hip. He must have done so without the safety on and while he was sleeping the gun discharged. The discharge of a gun that powerful had literally put a hole in the wall.

As I thought about this incident, I was wondering how the terrorists would actually react if the police felt they needed to strike the building to end the siege. Except for Khaalis, I didn't feel they would perform very well. I also knew the terrorists had a wide array of weapons and ammunition at their disposal. They had an advantage with the floor being barricaded and complete knowledge of what was happening on the 8th floor. I wasn't so naïve to think the terrorists would not fight the police if needed. The unknown of what would happen to us in a gun battle was an overwhelming feeling. I knew what was going on in front of me. The terrorists had not executed anyone and it was more stable for us than the first hours of the take over which were violent. It was easy to say to yourself, ok, let's keep this situation as level as possible. It became a natural thought to hope the police would not do anything rash. In actuality, these thoughts were not very realistic—but a bit of wishful thinking. We were still being threatened with death, the men were tied up, people had been injured and the odds of a successful conclusion probably were not in our favor.

CHAPTER TWENTY SIX

TOUGH NEGOTIATIONS

Through late Wednesday evening and the early hours of Thursday morning, Ambassador Zahedi continued to try and find common ground for a meaningful dialogue and negotiations with Khaalis. For his part Khaalis kept going back to his demands about the killers of his family being brought to him so he could provide the appropriate justice as well as the other demands he articulated. The ambassador would always temper his comments to Khaalis that he was not a representative of the police or U.S. government and could not personally deliver on any of those demands. He told him he wanted to listen and understand. During much of these conversations, Khaalis would accuse the ambassador of trying to stall him and trick him—the building of confidence and trust between them was not occurring.

At one point, Khaalis told the ambassador that he shouldn't fool himself that he would be able to bring the siege to a successful conclusion unless his demands were met. As he ended one of the conversations he told the ambassador to let the police know the only thing they would find on the 8th floor would be all of our ashes.

After this exchange, the ambassador, for the first time, started to have thoughts and feelings leading to a lessening in his confidence that the hostage siege would end without a significant loss of life. He and his ambassador counterparts were becoming disillusioned.

Ambassador Zahedi loved to tango. In fact he tangoed with some famous and beautiful women—he dated Elizabeth Taylor and Jackie Onassis at the same time, which any man would think was quite an accomplishment.

He used his love to tango as an analogy to his diplomatic work. He always said that it takes two to tango and just as in negotiations, it takes two people willing to discuss the issues and see where they can reach agreement and resolution. After spending time on the phone with Khaalis, Ambassador Zahedi was not sure that Khaalis really wanted to tango. Mullany and his negotiator colleague's perspective was the hostages were doing the right thing to keep alive. The plan all along was to keep it simple. Keep Khaalis talking, avoid controversy at all costs, keep him concerned about the people he was holding and also try to distract him from discussing the killing of his family. Mullany also knew the situation was incredibly volatile and circumstances were changing on a minute-to-minute basis.

If I had known the ambassador was speaking with Khaalis, I could have confirmed for him his feelings about the seriousness of Khaalis's threats to the police that they would find our ashes. My internal clock was telling me that it was about 1:00 am on Thursday when Khaalis made one of his appearances from the other side of the building. He came in specifically to tell us that the police couldn't use that psychological stuff on him, that it wasn't going to work, that he wouldn't be tricked. He also told us that the publicity he was receiving really didn't mean that much to him, that he didn't do this for publicity, that he did it for retribution. He wanted the killers of his family and he wanted other things done as well. The world had not listened to him, but it was too late to make amends for not listening before. He kept repeating the publicity he was receiving didn't matter to him, but at the same time would let us know the entire universe knew what was happening. People were calling from around the globe to talk with him. As Khaalis made these pronouncements his men would look at each other and smile. You could see they knew they were getting a tremendous amount of publicity, attracting international attention. You could see from the look in their faces and their body language that they were proud of their accomplishment.

During one of Khaalis's visits with us in our section of the floor, he encountered Eddie Mason, a painter working on the building and who was swept up in the hostage siege. Known to us as Eddie the Painter, he looked at Khaalis and told him that he wasn't scared of him and that if it was his time to die, it was his time to die. He did this as he was sitting on the floor and his hands tied behind his back. At first Khaalis seemed amused at

Eddie's pronouncements and then he just turned, grabbed a rifle from one of his men and hit Eddie with the butt of the rifle on the back of his head and knocked him unconscious. A number of the women started screaming at Khaalis not to kill him. He told his men to turn Eddie over on his stomach and they bent his legs up towards his head and tied his legs and hands together. For his act of defiance, Eddie was now hogtied in the middle of the room. He remained like that for some time. Eddie regained consciousness later and appeared groggy and uncomfortable. He was squirming around and Abdul Salaam, one of the terrorists who kept watch over us, put his foot on his back and told him to keep still. Eddie told him that he wasn't going to stay in that position so he might as well as pull the trigger.

When Khaalis returned to our area, he ordered his men to untie his legs. He told Eddie he admired him for his bravery and since he was not afraid to die, they'd keep him off to the side and use him as one of the first to be executed.

Perhaps he had reached a point where he just didn't care and that our circumstances were not going to get better so he might as well tell Khaalis exactly what he thought. For the rest of us, we thought silence was the better part of valor and remained quiet and obedient.

At one point in the middle of the night, Latif was sitting quietly in one of the chairs with his hand gun resting on his knee just looking from side to side at his hostages. He was slumped in his chair. The vast majority of us had not slept. Willing yourself to sleep to find some escape from what we were experiencing would have been nice, but wasn't realistic. From my perspective, the pain in my shoulders was a constant reminder of where we were. Sometime early Thursday morning, it must have been about 3:00, the terrorists rotated a few us from the front line to along the wall. Having an opportunity to place your back against a hard structure provided some relief from the pressure on your back and shoulders. It felt like I had won the lottery. I was looking directly at Latif as were others and he told us to stop staring at him with our sad eyes. He told us that such looks would not change our situation and we should accept our fate. Looking at him with eyes and expressions of helplessness would not save us.

Many of the calls coming into the B'nai B'rith Building were mostly for Khaalis from Deputy Chief Rabe. During one of these calls, Ambassador Zahedi had his colleague from Pakistan get on the phone. Khaalis's Islamic teacher with whom he had studied for 30 years had been from Pakistan. They spent about 30 minutes on the phone and Khaalis repeated his demands . Whatever they discussed it didn't resolve the crisis. After each call, the ambassadors would cover what had been discussed among themselves and the police. The creeping lack of confidence to help resolve the hostage siege among the ambassadors was getting stronger with each subsequent call with Khaalis. From his own perspective, Ambassador Zahedi was becoming more disheartened in the wee hours of Thursday morning though he knew he had to keep trying to find a way to save lives.

CHAPTER TWENTY SEVEN

WOULD YOU LIKE CREAM WITH THAT COFFEE AND HOW ABOUT A BATHROOM BREAK?

BJ was sitting with Khaalis as the sky started to lighten Thursday and she looked over at the clock and saw it was about 6:00 am. She thought how nice it would be to have a cup of coffee. She finally let her thoughts become a request and told Khaalis how much she would enjoy a cup of coffee. Khaalis looked at her and said he could arrange that. He instructed her to get Deputy Chief Rabe on phone. He had a conversation with Rabe and said he'd allow coffee to be sent up to the 8th floor for all the hostages. He also called his family and instructed his son-in-law to prepare food for him and his men. He told him to call police Captain O'Brien and arrange to get the food to the lobby of the B'nai B'rith Building so it would be sent up with the coffee for the hostages.

Since the siege had started at 11:00 am on Wednesday we had not received any nourishment. When someone went to the bathroom, they had a chance to grab sips of water at the water fountain, but that was the extent of any food and water. I had not thought much about food and water for the last 19 hours. I was more concerned about stopping my face from bleeding and not to bleed to death and focusing on positive thoughts on how I was going to survive. That's where I was putting my energies.

Throughout Wednesday afternoon and evening, I watched my male colleagues make their way to the men's room, going through the ritual the terrorists had established. If you couldn't get up by yourself, one of the older men would come over and help you to your feet. You'd head to a wall near the elevator bank and were met by one of the terrorists who put you against the wall at an angle with all the pressure on your neck. A rifle barrel was placed into your neck or the back of your head as your hands were untied. While you were being untied, you would be subjected to an anti-Semitic tirade. Many times the person was asked where he came from. We understood the meaning of the question. They didn't mean Silver Spring where I lived or Miami where I grew up. They meant the natural historical areas where the migration of Jews to the United States had taken place--from Eastern Europe, Russia, Germany, Prussia and other areas where pogroms had persecuted and killed Jews. We were told that we should go back to where we came from and that we had created all the ills of the world and we were nothing but filthy Jews. After you were untied, you were taken into the bathroom. After you were finished, you came back out and took the same position so that your hands could be retied. It still did not look like a very pleasant experience. I guesstimated it was about 3:00 am or 4:00 am Thursday and I had not been to the men's room for 17 or 18 hours. I still felt dehydrated but knew that I should try to go sooner or later since it was not doing my kidneys much good to have waited that length of time. I also was not that interested in taking a look at my face based on the continuing reaction from my colleagues on my appearance.

Finally, I decided it was time. I requested that I be allowed to go the bathroom. I was able to get to my knees and push myself up. I walked across the room where one of the terrorists met me and put me against the wall at a 45 degree angle with all the pressure on my head and neck. He put a long gauge shot gun in the nape of my neck and started to talk to me as he untied my hands.

Prior to getting up and walking over to the wall, I had already practiced in my mind what I would say when I was questioned on where I came from. When I was a kid growing up in Miami my paternal grandfather Herman use to kid me that if the boat to the U. S. from London, England, had been 25 cents more, I'd be a Limey today. Herman's real name was Hyman Greenfogel, and he was born in London in 1898. In 1904, when he was 6 years old, he immigrated to the U.S. with his parents Morris and Malke, my great grandparents, who I did not know, and his sister Jane,who I knew

126

as Aunt Jean. The ship, built in 1888, was 10,000 tons and named the City of New York. It had three funnels and three masts. Morris and Malke had left Russia to escape the pogroms and had made their way to England before getting to America. They landed at Ellis Island on November 13, 1904, to begin their new life. At times I thought Herman was joking with me. Years later, looking at the Ellis Island historical web site, I experienced one of those rare moments one has in life that can literally take your breath away. There on my computer screen was the record from Ellis Island for one Hyman Greenfogel. Born in 1898 and arriving at Ellis Island in 1904. And now, that joke that Herman use to tell me was going to be a basis for my answer to a question from a terrorist who wanted me to go back to where I came from. That's if I lived long enough to do so.

As he untied my hands, he told me that I should go back to where I came from,- how I and my fellow Jews had created all the ills of the world. He then asked me where I came from. He was expecting to hear what he had heard from all of my colleagues. From parts of the world where Jews had thrived as productive citizens in their country of birth and for many of them later to be persecuted for being Jewish and where many perished for their religious beliefs.

After his question, I quietly told him London, England– that my grandfather was from England. There was dead silence on his part. He actually was speechless. Having never imagined I would give him such a response, he didn't know how to respond to me. As I stood with my head against the wall with his rifle in the back of my neck I smiled to myself and silently thanked Herman for the wonderful story that I have told hundreds of times.

I turned to look at the terrorist and for the first time my hands were untied in 18 to 20 hours. The instant relief was wonderful. He told me to go into the bathroom and also suggested that I wash my face off since it was all crusted with blood. I asked him which bathroom I should use, the men's or the women's? I remembered Khaalis's admonitions Wednesday and recalled that he didn't want us to use the restroom he was using. The terrorist didn't respond to my question and as I walked down the short hall way I was confused and indecisive on which bathroom to use. I thought the women were still heading to the bathroom at the same time so I made a choice to use the men's room. I had already determined that I would make it a quick visit. I didn't want to run into one of the terrorists and found using the wrong facility. Seeing myself in the mirror for the first time, my face was swollen on the right side, crusted with blood, and I had a black eye that was spectacular. It was a deep black and covered my entire eye.

People who knew me always kidded that I looked like Joe Namath, the football great. My hair was fairly long and if I looked like Broadway Joe, he must have had a really bad game or played without his helmet. I washed my face and the water felt refreshing. As I looked at myself once again I thought it didn't look too bad.

I also made sure to wipe up the bathroom before I left. Luckily I didn't run into any terrorists so I never knew if I was standing in a place where I should not have been that might have had negative consequences.

I walked back to the wall area where the terrorist was waiting for me with my neck tie in his hand and reassumed the position—my head against the wall and feet extended behind me. He roughly pushed my elbows up as high as they would go behind my back and tightly retied my hands. He must have been thinking about what I told him and in his own way he was telling me that he didn't find it amusing. When I told my brother Barry what I had done since he heard the story many times as well, he filled me in on a fact I did not know. Prior to settling on America, Morris traveled independently to Argentina to look over the country as a haven for his family. He felt uncomfortable with the country and language and went back to England to gather his family, his decision made. I wonder what the terrorist's reaction would have been if I told him Argentina?

He turned me around and pushed me back towards where I had come from to lie back down on the floor. As I walked back I looked to my right where the women were lying and I smiled at a number of my colleagues and nodded my head. I found my spot and managed to get back to the ground without hitting my head on the floor. I thought that was a major accomplishment. As I lay back down, though my hands were once again tied behind my back, having gone to the bathroom and washing my face, I felt better. At least psychologically I did.

Later, a number of my women colleagues told me that when they saw me return, and the blood had been washed from my face, I seemed to have a lighter step in my walk. It actually lifted their spirits. Well, I was glad to have accomplished two goals. I proved to myself that my face was somewhat intact and propped up the hopes of colleagues.

The routine we went through to go to the bathroom also produced an interesting situation that might have been one of the first declarations of Gay Pride. One of our colleagues, Billy Clamp, who worked in the accounting area needed to go the restroom and proceeded to subject himself to the prescribed steps the terrorists required. When Billy got to the area where a terrorist waited and placed his head against the wall, the terrorist noticed that he had something in his pocket. Even at this stage, the terrorists were concerned that someone retained an item that could be used as a weapon against them. Before he untied Billy's hands, the terrorist reached into Billy's front pocket and pulled out a case of lipstick. The reaction was instantaneous. He loudly exclaimed what he found and called his fellow terrorists to see the lipstick case. He called Billy queer and other derogatory names.

As we all watched what was transpiring, we were concerned they would hurt Billy for his sexual orientation. To his credit, Billy retained his dignity and told the terrorists that he did use the lipstick. After awhile, they calmed down and let Billy go to the bathroom. He remained a bit of a cause celeb among the terrorists.

CHAPTER TWENTY EIGHT

DID YOU ADD A GRATUITY FOR THAT DELIVERY AND HANK'S SITUATION

As we were enduring the hostage siege inside the building the families of the hostages were trying to handle their emotions and concerns. Late Wednesday, the Foundry Methodist Church, which is located at the intersection of P and 16th Streets, where President Bill Clinton and his family worshipped at times, offered its services as a gathering area for families. It also allowed families to express concerns they were having. One concern expressed to police and other authorities was that family members who were hostages were not receiving prescribed medications for a variety of ailments and they were extremely concerned with each passing hour. There were also a number of medical doctors who knew they had patients being held and were also concerned for their well being. For example, a number of psychiatrists who were treating colleagues had contacted the police about their concerns. They were not sure how their patients would react and hold up under the stress of what they were facing. As word got out that coffee was being allowed up to the 8th floor, families with concerns were readying prescription drugs that they had hoped would be included in the delivery.

Khaalis had further discussion with Deputy Chief Rabe on how the logistics would work. An elevator would be sent down; the police would load the elevator with the coffee and send it up to the 8th floor. If any police were on the car they would be killed and hostages would be killed as well.

Khaalis made one of his appearances with us after he spoke with Rabe. It contained more anti-Semitic rants; we were all going to be killed; we

131

should continue to pray to whomever we prayed to since our time on earth was drawing to a close. He then announced that coffee and doughnuts were going to be sent up to the 8th floor. Such a monologue!

The tension levels among the terrorists started to go sky high as the delivery time approached. We were told to be absolutely quiet and not to move. Our two guards re-positioned themselves so they were facing the elevator bank; they had their weapons leveled at the elevator as did their fellow terrorists. All of their fire power was now directed at the elevators. You could hear their weapons clicking with rounds being chambered and pistols being cocked. The tension level among us increased tremendously as well. This was the first time during the hostage siege since we had been moved to the 8th floor that something to do with the elevators was happening and it was disquieting to say the least. Did the terrorists think the police were coming up in the elevators? Was this the beginning of the shoot out and killing of hostages that Khaalis had promised from the beginning when I first encountered him on the 2nd floor?

You could hear the gears of the elevator start to operate and see the terrorists tense up, each one aiming his weapon in that direction. If someone was measuring the breathing pattern of the hostages I doubt you would have seen any frosting on a glass. If my colleagues were like me, they were holding their breaths.

I heard the elevator advancing up the floors. It finally reached the top and the door slid open. The terrorists yelled for someone to check the top of the elevator and then I heard someone say it's clear and they lowered their weapons.

For the second time since the start of the siege, tension had played out over the elevator. I heard noise in the elevator and the shuffling of something. Boxes were being placed near the door way and we were told coffee and doughnuts had arrived. My first thought was that the Red Cross had provided the food but I believe our good friends at the Gramercy Inn had prepared the goodies for us. Latif carried out a large bag and placed it on the floor near the boxes of coffee and food. It was the accumulation of prescription drugs that family members had given to the police; hopeful their loved ones would soon be getting their needed medications.

Wednesday evening, every so often, BJ would ask Khaalis about Hank Siegel. She mentioned his heart condition, she was worried about him and heard Khaalis and Latif say that he was lying on a board in the middle of the room.

After the food arrived, Khaalis came back into the room and asked where the little man with the heart condition was. He told him to come front and center and had a brief conversation with Hank. He told Hank he was going to send him down in the elevator. He warned him if police were in the elevator when they opened the doors, he would be dead and that he had better start praying that no police were near the 8th floor.

He also asked Hank if he was going to die on him. "Don't you die on me," Khaalis admonished. "A heart attack is a dirty way to die. Let me cut your head off, it's quick and clean." Hank told Khaalis that he didn't think he was going to die. Once again they trained their fire power on the elevator door as it opened. Khaalis had Hank thank Allah for his life before he put Hank in the elevator and sent him down. Once again the tension in the room became intense as they directed all their weapons on the elevator and the drama played out.

Hank was met by medical personnel and taken to the hospital for a checkup and observation. For the police, this was the first opportunity to speak with someone who was up on the 8th floor. Others the police had spoken with—Wes and Brian from the 2nd floor landing or others who had barricaded themselves in other parts of the building—provided little information other than what had transpired in the initial stages of the siege. Finally, the police and FBI's were able to get an accurate snapshot of what was occurring on the 8th floor.

When they spoke with Hank, they showed him three pictures of people they thought were involved and he identified them. Then Hank asked them where the other four pictures were? That surprised them and it was at that moment they realized they were dealing with more terrorists. They had assumed that only three gunmen had entered the building and were making decisions and plans on those assumptions. Up until Thursday morning the authorities did not have all the pertinent facts. One can only wonder what actions the police might have taken thinking only three terrorists were up on the 8th floor and not the seven that were holding us. There is no question in my mind that Hank's release was a critical juncture for the police and FBI to have more accurate information to access the situation and to have a clearer picture of what was happening to the hostages.

Khaalis had now released a number of people. First on the 2nd floor including Wes and Brian, a few women and Alton Kirkland. A number of them had severe injuries and Hank looked like he was going to die on us momentarily. As I thought about these releases, it really didn't calm my apprehension on what might happen to us. I didn't take the releases as an act of kindness on Khaalis's part. If there was any kindness evident, he would just release us all. It became apparent to me that he didn't want anyone on the 8th floor to die on him. He was probably concerned about what the police's reaction might be if he told them he was sending a body down in the elevator. My conclusion was if that became a reality, police action in trying to rescue us would be initiated as quickly as possible.

After the coffee and doughnuts arrived, it was sometime before the terrorists started distribution–first to the women. The men remained tied. At first, I wasn't sure if the men would be so lucky to be included in the morning meal. After the women had been fed, they turned to the men. The older men, who had been singled out to die first and remained untied, were instructed to help feed the other men. As they worked among us, I could see the "older men" were tired and scared, yet showed incredible compassion to their colleagues. First, Horace Gold, who managed B'nai B'rith's mail room operations and publication distribution, was handling the doughnuts. Horace came over to me and offered up a doughnut. He ripped off a few pieces and fed them to me. I'm glad that I didn't choke on the size of the pieces he gave me. I was sure to thank Horace profusely for his kindness.

Bernie Simon was assigned to the coffee brigade. He approached and offered a few sips of coffee. I've always loved my coffee with a little cream and two Sweet and Low's. And now, here was Bernie kneeling in front of me with a black coffee. He tried to keep the cup from shaking and I took a number of sips. I truly hate black coffee and yet it was one of the best tasting coffees that I had ever enjoyed. Bernie and I smiled at one another and I thanked him for his help. He then moved on to the next person. Though not a hearty meal by any stretch of the imagination, the few pieces of doughnut and sips of coffee seemed to refresh me and I imagined some of my energy had been restored. We were in a critical situation where you didn't know what would happen from minute-to-minute so it never crossed my mind when my next meal would come and or what it might be. I was just happy to have had the ability to absorb the small morsels offered us.

About this same time, my shoulders felt like they had separated and the pain was extreme. The brief respite I had going to the men's room had quickly dissipated. I looked at Salaam who was watching us and asked if it would be possible to get some aspirin. I figured the worst that he could say was no and for me to be quiet. I was pleasantly surprised when he asked any of the women if they had any aspirin with them.

A young colleague named Vicki, whom I did not know well, offered me some aspirin that she had in her pocket. She came across to the men's side and knelt down next to me. I'm not sure I ever had a chance to truly thank her for her kindness and gentleness. She was an attractive young woman with straight hair and I noticed how long her fingers were. She took two Daytril from her pocket and gave me one at a time which I swallowed without water. I was hoping that my words and eyes were expressing my appreciation. A short time later, the Daytril started to work and I noticed that the medication had taken an edge off the pain.

Latif turned his attention to the large bag of medicines that had been delivered with the food. An interesting situation created in a hostage setting is that information about one's personal life can be exposed to many people. I looked at the large bag and realized I had many colleagues who had various conditions that required medications.

Being 27 years old, I was in relatively good health and the only medication I took was an occasional aspirin for a strained muscle. I knew that Janie didn't have any medicine to send up to me, but I was truly hopeful she had given the police a chocolate Mr. Goodbar. I would have loved one and was disappointed when Latif didn't pull one out with my name on it.

Latif started to go through the large array of medicines. One relative actually sent a young woman her birth control pills. What was she thinking? It actually brought a laugh from a number of us when Latif announced what kind of medication it was. He was scrutinizing a number of the medicines very carefully and determined that he was not going to dispense some of them since they were strong narcotic or psychotherapeutic medicines. He was concerned that some people might try and utilize the drugs to commit suicide to escape the horrors they were facing. He was also becoming annoyed at this task and was quickly losing interest in trying to dispense the medications. In the end, not many people received the help that was sent by their relatives. I was still thinking about the Mr. Goodbar. I swore to myself that was one of the first things I was going to enjoy when I got out of this situation.

CHAPTER TWENTY NINE

THURSDAY, MARCH 10TH

As the city was awakening Thursday morning, BJ got busier. The phone lines began to light up once again with reporters calling Khaalis on the seven lines. One reporter asked Khaalis how he could believe the police. Another radio reporter suggested to him that the police were trying to trick him and that the police had sharp shooters positioned on buildings across from the B'nai B'rith Building and around the back. Khaalis was becoming enraged as the morning was becoming brighter.

At the same time, Ambassador Zahedi and his colleagues were trying to build rapport and trust with Khaalis on the phone which was becoming ever more difficult with the competing calls from reporters. Khaalis would erupt at Ambassador Zahedi and also accuse him of trying to trick him and not being honest with him. Ambassador Zahedi thought to himself that he had never had such conversations in his diplomatic career. He and his colleagues had entered a crisis of confidence stage. Ambassador Zahedi had not slept now for almost two days and had endured a trip across the Atlantic. He was tired and disillusioned. His two ambassador colleagues, Yaqub-Khan and Ghorbal, also were tired and had the same lack of confidence in their ability to help bring the hostage siege to a successful conclusion.

The three ambassadors had a conversation after their recent discussion with Khaalis and Yaqub-Kahn and Ghorbal indicated they were tired and needed to handle other things and see their family members. They weren't sure their continued involvement would make a difference. The ambassadors were growing tired of listening to Khaalis's rants and references to the Koran. Ambassador Zahedi urged them to remain involved and keep trying. He suggested they rest a few hours, take care of what they needed to do and then to come back and reengage with Khaalis. They agreed to do so.

As the coffee and doughnuts were being enjoyed, and we were making the best of it, you could actually feel a more lightened mood. Then Khaalis came back into the room and it was apparent that he was agitated. He was strident in his words and actions. The mood changed quickly and the other terrorists adopted his more belligerent behavior as well. The reporter who had asked him if he could trust the police and the one who asked him if he knew police snipers were across the street really set him off. He told us "They think they can trick me but they are wrong." Once again he emphasized that we would all be killed. Khaalis added that if the police hurt any of his men, he would start killing us and the police would learn he was serious about his demands. He told his men he learned the police had re-established snipers across the street and he was going to give them something to shoot at. His men were very nervous at this latest news. He told his men to get ready. The terrorists were looking through the cracks in the paint and paper that covered the windows to see if they could see the police snipers.

Latif was standing near the windows, looking out as well. He had learned my colleague Jay Manchester's name with his involvement on the work crews and called Jay over by name and had him stand next to him. He told Jay that he was going to help him string a number of the older men upside down to give the snipers something to shoot at. As Jay stood with Latif, Khaalis had gone back to his command center to have BJ place a call to Deputy Chief Rabe. He wanted the chief to know they knew there were snipers across the street and they had better remove them or he was going to start killing hostages and putting them in the windows upside down. He told Rabe that he'd also target 10 hostages for execution. Rabe told Khaalis he would take care of it and Khaalis told him he better be quick about it.

As Latif waited he decided that it was time to not only have the men's hands tied behind their backs but to have their feet tied up as well. He located rope and wire left over from the construction workers and began to tie men's feet.

Rabe must have convinced Khaalis the snipers would be removed and it would be done quickly for a short time later, Khaalis came back into our area and told his men the shooting was off for now and they'd just kill people later. He turned around and walked back out of the room. To say the tension in the room from went from pretending we were at a café enjoying coffee and doughnuts to a feeling of dread would have been an understatement. It was like a hit in the stomach that took your breath away. It was a wake-up call that our lives were still in danger.

As Washington woke up to Thursday, the families of those of us being held were facing another day of uncertainty and anxiety. The Foundry Methodist Church would be a bee hive of activity of families gathering and waiting to hear some positive news. I don't know how she did it, and to this day she can't recall how it happened, but somehow my wife Jane ended up at the Gramercy Inn next door to the B'nai B'rith Building. She said she wanted to get as close as possible to me and she certainly accomplished that goal. She must have talked her way past police blockades and walked over to the hotel. As a result she was able to observe police activity during most of Thursday.

CHAPTER THIRTY

TOUGH NEGOTIATIONS CONTINUE

At the police command center, the Ambassadors were back together after Yaqub-Khan and Ghorbal had taken a few hours' break. Now, Zahedi, Yaqub-Khan and Ghorbal would try and re-establish a positive dialogue with Khaalis. The conversations resumed and remained difficult with Khaalis not trusting the police and accusing the ambassadors of trying to trick him. None of his demands had been met and he was becoming impatient. At this point, Ambassador Zahedi didn't feel they were having success trying to develop a trusting relationship with Khaalis over the phone. The Ambassador had always relied on face- to-face negotiations. You could look into the eyes of the person you were negotiating with and judge how you were doing adjusting your words and even the rhythm on how you were delivering them. The person you were speaking with could also observe that you were being sincere and speaking from your heart. Ambassador Zahedi told Police Chief Cullinane that he really needed to meet with Khaalis face-to-face. Cullinane told Ambassador Zahedi that option would not even be considered and he wouldn't allow it. End of conversation. State Department officials also agreed with Cullinane's assessment and were not in favor of letting the ambassador go into the B'nai B'rith Building to meet Khaalis. Zahedi pressed the chief and Cullinae told him he would not put the three ambassador's lives at risk. Ambassador Zahedi was determined not to let what he perceived to be a need to meet Khaalis face-to-face for negotiations to be rejected out of hand by Cullinane; he continued to press his idea and gain acceptance. He was putting in perspective the situation in which he was a participant. He remembered the terrible shock when his grandmother died. He remembered when his beloved father, an important guide in life to him, was arrested by the British and held for three years. When he finally saw his father after his release, he was shocked by his appearance. Now, he was immersed in the first major hostage incident in the United States. He saw what the city of Washington, for which he also had a deep affection, looked like under siege and his shock mirrored how he had felt about his grandmother and father. Though he never considered himself a religious man by definition, Ambassador Zahedi had a very strong belief in God. He felt that something was pushing him to be involved and to use his abilities to try and save lives. Ambassador Zahedi fully realized he was putting his life at risk by wanting to see Khaalis face-to-face. He thought the risk was warranted since a feeling in his heart told him if he and his fellow ambassadors were not successful in their pleas to Khaalis the rescue plan he heard being discussed among the police authorities would result in the loss of many lives.

CHAPTER THIRTY ONE

IT DIDN'T SEEM TO BE GETTING BETTER

After Khaalis told his men the shooting was off, the tension level on the 8th floor subsided and that atmosphere was to last for a few hours. During that time, we talked the terrorists into letting the men, one at a time, stand up, have their hands untied and relieve the pain of having their elbows pushed up high towards their shoulders and their hands tied behind their backs for an extended period of time. Latif found a piece of chalk and came towards the left center of the room. He drew a circle and said that's where the men, one at a time, would stand. He also sternly informed us that if you were untied and you stepped outside the circle you would be killed. As with the bathroom, a number of people were content to pass on singling themselves out from the larger numbers of the group—they didn't want to be noticed by the terrorists. Being anonymous in this situation was not a bad thing. I fully understood the mood of the terrorists could change instantly and you could be out there all alone during a mood change and the consequences could be deadly. In spite of that threat, I eagerly awaited my turn to once again be untied to stretch my shoulders. I thought the risk was worth the reward. When my turn came, my hands were untied, my necktie was placed in my pocket and I also was able to reclaim my wallet and put it in my back pocket. After a short time of relief, Latif came over to tell me my time was up. He then retied my hands with my necktie and told me to go back and lie down. It was now over 24 hours since the building had been attacked and most of the men's hands been tied behind their backs for that period of time except for a few minutes to go the restroom and what they just allowed us to do.

A short time later, Latif initiated a new twist for the men to experience. First, he found a large empty paint bucket from the construction area. He started at the opposite side from me and I watched him drag each male colleague up to their feet one at a time. With a smile he told us we should experience what he and his fellow terrorists had experienced at the hands of the police—being frisked. He then spread each person's feet out and ran his hands from your ankles up each leg to your waist and checked around your waist. He checked your pockets to see if you had anything in them. If you had folded money in your pocket he took it out, refolded it and put it back in your pocket. Most people I knew including me, carried a wallet in their back pocket. He then removed your wallet and threw it into the bucket. The whole exercise was a bit disturbing. Not the notion of being frisked, though he was right I had never been frisked by a policeman. But what was he doing with our wallets? I related the taking of our wallets to the beginning of the siege when the terrorists did not want to know your name or develop any kind of relationship with the people they were holding. When Si Cohen went to the restroom he took out his wallet to show the terrorist next to him pictures of his family. He told him he wanted to see them again, hopeful they would relate to wanting to see a family and perhaps show some sympathy to the hostages' plight. The terrorist didn't care and told him to put his wallet away since having a family would not change the situation—he was going to be killed. When Latif got to me, he frisked me, took the few dollars I had in my pocket and refolded it and placed in my right front pocket. He noticed that I still had my watch on my left wrist and asked if I wanted it off. I said yes since it had been cutting into my wrist since having my hands tied. He was able to slip it over my left wrist and place it in the front left pocket of my pants. I had concluded why Latif was taking our wallets. I believed they had found a way to identify people to be killed. To have as much as a democratic process as possible, they would pick out a wallet and viola; they would have the person to be executed. Early Thursday afternoon, March 10, 1977 no one could have convinced me otherwise as to the intended purpose of the bucket with wallets.

Throughout Thursday Khaalis continued to have dialogue with the police, the ambassadors and reporters. No significant progress had been achieved and Ambassdaor Zahedi continued to press his case with Chief Cullinane to meet face-to-face. Cullinane remained steadfast in his refusal. Mid-afternoon, the police were able to suggest that additional food and drink be made available for the hostages. Making such suggestions was part of the strategy developed. The negotiating team wanted to distract Khaalis's thoughts away from his family's killing and have him concentrate on other details. Mullany and his colleagues at the Command Center felt they were succeeding in this effort. After awhile Khaalis agreed. As was the case with coffee and doughnuts, it took some time to work out the delivery logistics. We had no idea that these negotiations were going on; we were watching the mood of the terrorists jump around like a ball in a pin ball machine.

All of a sudden we felt the tension level rise unexpectedly. The terrorists told everyone to be quiet and they positioned themselves around the elevator bank. As with prior times, when anything played out around the elevators, that's where they focused all of their fire power. Once again, from the hostages perspective, we thought the police were making their move and a firefight was about to occur. We heard the elevator move and it came up to the 8th floor, opened up, heard a commotion and then the familiar all clear signal from the terrorists. As with the coffee and doughnuts Khaalis did not make an announcement that food was being delivered to the 8th floor. Latif and a few other terrorists were carrying out an array of boxes and placing them at the far end of the room near the elevator bank. There were quite a few more boxes than had been delivered that morning. It took them about 15-20 minutes to unload the elevator. My thinking was that the police thought they wouldn't have a lot of opportunities to get food to us and they were going to take advantage of Khaalis's offer and load up the elevator with as much food as they could. As he was taking out box after box, Latif was becoming more annoyed. He looked at us after bringing out a box and said "This is going to stop. I'm not going to keep bringing food to you people. What do you think I am a caterer?" He sounded like he was losing his patience and whatever sense of humor he brought into the building at 11:00 am on March 9th. It was not a good sign.

CHAPTER THIRTY TWO

THE COMMAND CENTER AND RISING TENSIONS

The ongoing dialogue with Khaalis from the police command center produced no breakthrough and the mood among police and the ambassadors remained bleak. Knowing the mercurial nature of Khaalis and that his demands, beyond the stopping of the movie, were not realistic, it was only natural for the police to develop alternative plans that required force to rescue us.

Back at the Gramercy, Jane had remained at the hotel. The police were discussing the elements of a potential rescue attempt in front of family members. The plan they were developing involved placing a SWAT team on the roof of the B'nai B'rith Building. They would use satchel charges and blow a hole in the roof that would allow them to drop into the 8th floor and confront the terrorists. In addition, another group would break through the door on the roof and use explosives to clear a path through the debris and make their way to the 8th floor. A third component was for SWAT members to rappel from the roof and crash through the windows facing Rhode Island Avenue. They were calculating casualty figures among the police and hostages. They would need to shoot to kill the terrorists. As Jane heard these discussions she became upset. Other relatives also over heard the plans and began to argue with the police that such a plan would be foolish and lead to the death of their loved ones. Jane thought that perhaps I wouldn't be coming home and she decided it was time to leave the Gramercy.

As this discussion was proceeding, Mullany knew this plan most likely would lead to a disaster for the hostages and the officers who would carry it out. Mullany sought out Don Bassett, the SWAT commander at the B'nai B'rith Building. He reiterated that a negotiated settlement was a necessity and the SWAT plan seemed like a suicide mission. The police felt a huge frustration coming up with a good tactical plan in case a rescue attempt was required. In the end, the plan that was developed was the plan that would be implemented.

Ambassador Zahedi was concerned about the consequences of blowing a hole in the roof and remained convinced the loss of life among the hostages would be astronomical. He thought it would be a blood bath and he was very disturbed. The ambassador was also worried about the arrival that afternoon of the British Prime Minister James Callaghan who was to be greeted by President Carter at the White House.

Under normal circumstances when a visiting head of state arrived he was afforded a 19 gun salute with cannons that were positioned on the mall just south of the White House. Ambassador Zahedi became very concerned the cannons would set off Khaalis and lead him to think the police were attacking him. First the ambassador called his friend Peter Jay, the Ambassador from Britain who was also Prime Minister Callaghan's son-in-law. He told him that he was going to make a call to National Security Advisor Zbigniew Brzezinski to request that the 19 gun salute not be done in deference to what was happening in the city and he wanted Ambassador Jay to apologize on his behalf to the Prime Minister. Jay told him he understood and would convey his thoughts to his father-in-law.

Ambassador Zahedi made his calls. On a parallel track, police officials made a call to Jody Powell, Carter's Press Secretary at the White House and told him of their concern. Powell agreed with the assessment. The Army cannoneers were already positioned on the Mall. Powell was able to make contact with them and instructed them to return to their base back in Virginia. They loaded up the Howitzers, boarded busses and left. Powell then briefed President Carter. He became furious the order had been given. He didn't want a message being sent the U.S. would give into terrorists. He told Powell to reverse the order. By shear timing, they were not able to contact the soldiers and have them turn around. The 19 gun salute did not occur when the Prime Minister arrived at the White House to see President

Carter. In his mind, Ambassador Zahedi averted a potential disaster for the hostages. It was decided Rabe would tell Khaalis the truth about the cannons and any potential gun fire heard did not involve any of the buildings where his men were holding hostages. One could only imagine the reaction of Khaalis and the terrorist's at all three buildings if they heard the sounds of guns going off. At this stage of the siege they were incredibly nervous and tense. From my perspective it would not have taken much to produce a negative reaction with serious consequences for us.

The negotiations between the ambassadors and Khaalis remained stymied. For the first time, Ambassador Zahedi suggested to Khaalis they meet face-to-face. Khaalis remained silent briefly and said he'd have to think about it. The building of trust between the ambassadors, police and Khaalis was still a delicate situation.

CHAPTER THIRTY THREE

THURSDAY GETS TOUGHER

After the food arrived, the terrorists distributed the sandwiches and sodas to the women first. It was mid-afternoon on Thursday. Once again I thought the food had been arranged through the Red Cross but I subsequently learned the food had been prepared by the Washington Hilton Hotel. Perhaps they remembered a number of us who worked closely with them during the B'nai B'rith Convention in September of 1976.

I'm not sure what was transpiring on the other side of the floor in Khaalis's command center, but something was up since the mood among the terrorists was changing. At first it was just slightly perceptible and then it came across in bigger waves. They stopped distributing the food to the women. I did not take that as a positive sign but couldn't figure out what had created this change of heart. Based on Latif's actions, I always took him to be the second in command. He gave orders to other terrorists that were followed. He was becoming more upset with us as well. At one point, standing in the middle of the room as if he was just talking to himself, he uttered it was time for Khaallis to stop fooling everyone. He needed to come in and tell all these people what's really up. My interpretation of his words was unsettling and I feared something bad was going to happen. After his comments, Latif disappeared around the corner to see Khaalis.

As he continued discussions with the police and the ambassadors, Khaalis reiterated his demands and expressed his annoyance that all this talk was just to trick him. While speaking with the police, he also handled calls with reporters, his family and the other two buildings. On Thursday afternoon, Khaalis's own perception about police intentions must not have been positive either. Perhaps he thought the police were trying to trick him and lull him into complacency. I can only guess that Latif's comments to Khaalis added to his apprehension.

From the time they relocated all the hostages to the 8th floor, the terrorists would hear the various noises a building emits; some made them more nervous than others. If they heard something they considered out of the ordinary they assumed it was related to police activity and a rescue attempt. One of my captured colleagues who I knew as John was the assistant to the building's chief engineer Bernie Sullivan who was not held hostage. Unfortunately, Bernie's daughter who worked at B'nai B'rith, was captured and held on the 8th floor. The terrorists learned John's position during the early stages and used his knowledge as they stopped stairwells. They also gained an understanding of roof access and other ways in and out of the `building. They questioned him about the causes of the noise. John told them it was the compressor going off and on and that would satisfy them. Late afternoon on Wednesday a loud thump came from the roof. It was so pronounced no one on the 8th floor could ignore it. Everyone's eyes went to the ceiling and there was total silence in the room. Maybe my ears were playing tricks on me but I also heard footsteps on the roof immediately after the thump. No question in my mind the two sounds were related. The plan of action that Jane over heard and Ambassador Zahedi knew the police were formulating must have had an opening stage for implementation and the curtain had parted on act one. When it occurred, Latif was sitting in a chair and his eyes went to the ceiling along with the other terrorists. He jumped up, his eyes got wide and he gripped his gun tighter. He looked around the room and spotted John and said with as much sarcasm he could put in his voice, "So John, what did you think that sound was, the compressor?" Almost in unison we yelled out "Yes, it was the compressor." Latif was standing and still looking at ceiling when he proclaimed quite excitedly, "The compressor—like hell." He actually had a smile on his face. As he finished his statement, we all began to laugh. If you had only a sliver of sense of humor left in you even after what we had already experienced, you couldn't help but laugh as you listened and watched what had played out over the last few minutes.

Latif quickly left the room to consult with Khaalis. He came back sometime later with a renewed determination and conviction. The humor of the previous moment had passed quickly and we could see he was serious and no longer smiling. He came back to finish what he had started earlier in the day. Unfortunately, it wasn't to restart the distribution of food. He instructed the terrorists to immediately begin tying all the men's feet. It didn't take me long to remember what Khaalis had said about tying our feet. I replayed it in my head verbatim: "Tie up the men's feet good, we don't want them bunny hopping around when the shooting starts." That's what he said. The logic of what I heard was fairly simple to follow. When you tie up our feet, it was a good chance that shooting was to start and people were going to be killed. The tension in the room took off like a rocket. The rhetoric that we heard since 11:00 am on Wednesday–that we were going to die–had intensified to a believable level. The terrorists had twine, rope and insulated wire that they used to methodically tie the men's feet. For the first time in the siege, all the men's hands and feet were tied. During the process, the terrorist would look you in the eye, smile, and tell you that you would be killed in their holy war. When my feet were tied, the feeling of helplessness just washed over me. It was bad enough when my hands were tied behind my back; having my feet tied magnified the feeling beyond what my mind was able to comprehend. Throughout the entire siege, I would look at little signs; the release of Wes and Brian on the 2nd floor; Hank's release on Thursday morning; and the allowing of food to be delivered on Thursday morning and afternoon. They were signs that I could point to that everything had a chance to work out in the end. When our feet were tied, I could find no redeeming explanation that would give me hope. Khaalis's comment that he didn't want us bunny hopping around when the shooting started did not resonate with me. With my feet tied, I realized that it would not take great effort for the terrorists to kill us as they had promised from the outset. For the first time they also cut off trips to the bathroom for women as well. They told people to stop talking. The terrorists thought a police action to rescue us was starting and they were getting ready for a fire fight with them. If you were to poll my colleagues after we heard the thump, the vast majority of them would have concurred with that conclusion.

I knew the anxiety level among my colleagues was increasing at this time as well. As they were tying our feet, Norman Buckner called out to the terrorists asking if we could talk about their demands. Couldn't we make a phone call to the authorities to speak on their behalf? One of the terrorists yelled over to him to shut up. He said that it was too late to ask any questions; now was the time everyone was going to die. I could see that Norman was upset and probably thinking we didn't have much time left. Norman's statements seemed quite naïve and foolish to the terrorists. They also had a hint of a fatalistic tone to them. The atmosphere and mood on the 8th floor was sinking fast. The thump on the roof proved to me the police were not just sitting back and waiting for some kind of conclusion. For whatever reasons that I was not privy to, they had escalated their activity and whether they knew it or not, that had inflamed the terrorists. As I lay on the floor with my hands and feet tied, I was hoping and praying the police were not about to do something stupid that might kill us.

What intersection of variables was bringing the hostage siege to this point? Was it a concern for Khaalis's constant insistence about his demands that the police knew were unrealistic to meet? That they needed to be in position if time ran out and Khaalis started to kill hostages as promised? Was it the information from Hank's release that they were dealing with more terrorists and the conditions that existed on the 8th floor? Or was it a lack of confidence in the ambassadors' and police's ability to negotiate a peaceful conclusion? The authorities obviously were working a two track solution to the crisis. Continue to negotiate and also put into place the resources that were necessary to free us with force even with the realization that numerous hostages and police might be killed.

We had not seen Khaalis for some time Thursday afternoon when he returned to our area as his men were tying our feet. He looked around and told his men to make sure they were tight so they would not become undone during the shooting. Then he turned and walked out of the room.

The terrorists who remained were tense and nervous, though focused on their surroundings. Since it was still light outside, they stood by the cracks in the paint and cardboard on the windows and scanned the outside. They remained concerned about snipers across the street at the Holiday Inn and they could also see activity on Rhode Island Avenue just below. After our feet were tied we were instructed to flip over and remain on our stomachs.

For the first time, they told the women they needed to lie flat down on the floor on their stomachs as well.

The noise from the roof and whatever was transpiring with Khaalis in his command center also precipitated actions from the terrorists that I had not observed before. Each of them was carrying a rifle; before some of them just had handguns. I had not seen some of the weaponry they were displaying. In addition, each of the terrorists had an ammunition bag with a strap that went over their head and would rest at their side. This new accessory had been added to make it easier for them to reload as they fought the police. To watch this development was unsettling to say the least. As I looked at other colleagues, my new thoughts were not singular in nature but shared by others who were taking in what my senses were clearly telling me.

CHAPTER THIRTY FOUR

THURSDAY, MARCH 10TH. DAY TURNS TO NIGHT AND WITH DARKNESS, MORE DESPAIR

As Thursday started to turn to twilight, the tension level on the 8th floor was severe. The terrorists were adamant that there be no talking among ourselves–they wanted the room silent. They also wanted everyone to remain on their stomachs. The terrorist's nervousness was apparent and as I watched them, I wondered, what are they thinking? Their actions pointed towards a belief the police were going to attack the building to try and free us. Did they really think they could fight them and be successful based on the resources the police would employ?

For almost 30 hours those of us who were being held hostage could not help to have thoughts that we might be killed. It occurred to me that they might have thoughts similar to the people they had victimized and brutalized. An answer to this thought would come a few hours later and it was unsettling.

As darkness settled in, the terrorist's vigilance in keeping their weapons at the ready did not subside. They also were patrolling areas of the room on the other side of the 8th floor where they had not patrolled before. I began to think that this new crisis was building and it would be severe. The sense of stability that we might have enjoyed earlier Thursday was broken.

I noticed Latif standing by the opening to the 8th floor near the elevator bank. He looked like he was on a mission and fulfilling a purpose. I could see that he had a small note pad and pen. He stopped and wrote a short note on the pad, ripped it off and tucked it in his shirt pocket. Then he gave each of the terrorists the pad and waited while they wrote a short note and placed it in their shirt pockets. It was clear to me the terrorists had just written a note to Allah to be found on their bodies after they had been killed by the police. This was the answer to my thought about what the terrorists were thinking. When they first entered the building on Wednesday what else could they have been thinking? Did they really believe that Khaalis's demands would be met, particularly bringing his family's killers to him? If they did, that was an irrational thought. If they knew such demands were unreasonable, then the end game had to be martyrdom for their cause. Their deaths must have been contemplated before they entered the B'nai B'rith Building. Writing the note was an affirmation that the time had arrived.

After writing the notes, one of the terrorists sat down in a chair on the right side of the room and busied himself with a project. At first I didn't understand what he was doing and then it fascinated me. He placed his carbine rifle next to his chair and put the ammunition bag next to his chair as well. He also had an adhesive tape dispenser. He took out an ammunition clip shaped like a banana and then took out a similar ammunition clip. He crossed the two clips and placed them on his lap, ripped off a piece of tape with his teeth and then taped the clips together. I had never served in the military (having received a high draft number when the lottery was conducted during the Vietnam War) though I recognized he was handling ammunition clips. I was trying to figure out what he was doing. My "ah ha" moment came when he placed the crossed clip into his carbine. Each banana clip contained 32 rounds. By crossing the clips and taping them, he could fire off 64 rounds without having to reach for another. I watched him cross every round in the bag. His doing this, the notes each of them wrote and put in their pockets and their general demeanor provided all the proof I needed—they thought the police were going to try and rescue us. They were prepared to battle the police and were prepared to die.

If Ambassador Zahedi was suffering a periodic loss of confidence during the tense and delicate negotiations, my confidence that we'd survive this ordeal was being challenged greatly as well.

After the initial stages of the siege when we were finally grouped on the 8th floor there was some joking among ourselves to keep up our spirits that everything would turn out ok. In spite of the grave situation, many of us had not lost our sense of humor. But when this new crisis started on Thursday, the joking waned and by late afternoon had essentially stopped. For the first time in 30 hours, we were left with our own thoughts. It wasn't hard to visualize; the holy war Khaalis had been lecturing us about since Wednesday morning was about to become a reality. As I looked at the terrorists, I wondered how they would actually react if the police indeed came through the roof and made their way up the stairwells to fight for our freedom. Would they direct their firepower at the police or would decide they were going to die and turn their guns on us? We were easy targets, especially the men with hands and feet tied. We weren't going anywhere. I was particularly concerned that since a number of the younger terrorists were not as disciplined as Khaalis or Latif they would take a number of us with them. This prospect was dreadful and one over which we had no control. If shooting started, I didn't believe that Khaalis would be able to control or direct his men. It would be chaos in a confined area and was sure the police would be sending in ample numbers of SWAT team members to overwhelm the terrorists. After Hank's release they now knew how many terrorists they had to neutralize and an idea of the difficult challenges they were facing once the decision was made. At this stage, I started to give some thought to how many of us were going to be killed.

As it got darker outside, I estimated that it was about 7:00 pm. We had now been tied hand and feet and told to remain quiet for over three hours. As the evening moved on, Latif sat in a chair near the elevator bank. I was struck by his calmness. With his pistol in his hand he chatted with one of the other terrorists. He seemed serene. This was not reassuring. Latif must have reached a state of mind that he knew his fate and had accepted it. Throughout the hostage siege, I observed Latif's actions, manner and his interaction which was pragmatic. This was not to diminish the fact that he was one of the perpetrators of the siege and that he had physically assaulted my colleagues and constantly threatened us with death. Now he just looked like a man, no longer in control of the situation, who was prepared to take whatever came. A short time later, that serene nature did evaporate. I had overestimated his state of mind.

The dread and tension among the hostages early Thursday evening was the highest it had ever been during the entire siege. Throughout the last 30 hours we, through quiet words, barely perceptible nods of the head and expressions through our eyes, gave support and encouragement to one another.

Now, that group encouragement became more of a solitary groping of controlling emotions and convincing oneself that you were going to survive and see your family again and enjoy the life you envisioned for the future. The simple mentality that existed, at least among the men, was based on survival. You were either convincing yourself that you were going to see Friday arrive or wondering how it might feel to be killed.

At this juncture, the men had managed to bunch themselves along the wall so there was a single line interrupted by pillars. If we could have burrowed into the cement to form a protective cover, we would have done so. I had determined that I was going to survive and even being tied up, I told myself what to do and passed along my thoughts to colleagues close by. When the shooting started I could possibly survive a gunshot wound on the right side of my body away from my heart. I would lie on my left side and keep the right side of my body exposed. This technique was passed along the wall and quietly discussed among the men. If someone had taken a picture it would have looked like a shark's fin with everyone keeping their left side down and right side up.

I couldn't fathom what my colleagues were thinking to themselves–I only knew my thoughts. Human nature being such, one wished, hoped and prayed that it would be you who survived. I'm not sure what pressures the human experience could take, physically and psychologically, to think otherwise. Were my thoughts similar to what a solider feels when he or she is in a battle? I also tried to rationalize in a positive way comments the terrorists were making.

Standing near us were two of the youngest terrorists armed with carbine rifles with their crossed banana clips in their weapons. One said, "You shoot them in the head and I'll shoot them in the legs." I made a leap of faith in assuming they were speaking about the SWAT Team members. Police would be wearing protective vests and they would need to aim at more vulnerable parts of their bodies. I said to myself, that's what they meant. As I became comfortable with this assessment, one of the terrorists who just had this conversation pointed his rifle towards us and moved it up and down the line along the wall like he was shooting each of us. The prospect that one of the younger terrorists, who thought he was going to be killed, would let his hostages go to waste didn't make sense. He would take as many of us with him as possible. I know they thought they were going to meet Allah. I wanted to go home and see Jane and Emily and eat that Mr. Goodbar I wanted so badly that morning which seemed like such a long time ago compared to the 12 hours that had just passed.

During this time one of our colleagues, Norman Feingold, became unruly. Norman, the Director of B'nai B'rith's Career and Counseling Department, was a highly respected expert in his field. He had a bit of a reputation internally as an eccentric and someone who worked within his own world. He had been identified as one of the older men to be executed first and though his hands were tied behind his back, for some reason they must have missed him when they tied all the men's feet.

As I looked over my shoulder Norman was standing and talking loudly. He started walking around the room and as Latif noticed this he went ballistic. He stared to yell at Norman to get back down on the floor. Norman just ignored him and continued to walk around the room, speaking loudly. What he was saying made no sense to us but maybe it did to him. Latif had his pistol in his hand and was pointing it at Norman, screaming at him to stop walking around and to get back down on the floor or he was going to kill him. My only thought was that Norman had suffered a breakdown and wasn't in control of his faculties. A number of us saw this situation turning bad—that Latif was serious about killing Norman. Latif became more agitated with each passing minute and was getting closer to Norman. A number of us were also yelling at Norman to get back down on the floor. He ignored our pleas as well. As the situation reached a crescendo, we made a suggestion to Latif to find a long piece of wood and then take one of the chairs they were sitting in, put Norman in the chair and then put the wood underneath one arm of the chair, thread it through Norman's arms which were tied behind his back and out through the other side. Latif stopped moving toward Norman apparently considering the suggestion. He told another terrorist to go to the far side of the room where the construction materials were piled. He came back with a fairly long piece of wood that was rounded and looked like a pole. Latif did exactly what was suggested. He placed Norman in the chair, slipped the pole under the arm rest through his tied hands and out the other side. Norman tried to stand up and couldn't–mission accomplished. The question as to whether Latif would have killed Norman was moot. Based on the tension levels early Thursday evening and Latif's mood, the odds that Latif might have crossed into a point of no return and killed Norman were high.

A short time later, restrained Norman was sound asleep while the rest of us had frayed nerve endings. The Norman Feingold incident, as it became known among colleagues, truly was a scary affair. We had witnessed a breakdown and I wondered if there had been a prescription in that bag that came up with the coffee some 12 hours ago that had Norman's name on it.

Early Thursday evening, the police were reviewing their options. They brought together the police commanders in charge of each of the buildings to assess the circumstances. If a decision was made, it would have to be a coordinated effort at the three buildings. They couldn't chance a rescue at one building knowing that news would reach the others and cause a reaction from the terrorist furthering endanger the hostages. The police were fairly confident they could extract the hostages from the District Building and the Islamic Center within a short time frame and do so without endangering them. The three commanders were taking a hard look at the B'nai B'rith Building and trying to determine the odds for success without a substantial loss of life. They walked parts of the building that were accessible, noting the stairwells that were blocked with debris. They took a helicopter ride around the building to get a further sense of the challenges they were facing in a rescue attempt. The conclusions they were reaching were far from encouraging. It was becoming more obvious that lives would be lost if an assault on the B'nai B'rith Building was going to be the only viable option. We were the problem and the focus on a negotiated settlement became more important.

As the police evaluation was progressing, Ambassador Zahedi remained convinced the only way to proceed in trying to negotiate a successful conclusion was to meet face-to-face with Khaalis. He had raised this with Khaalis earlier and though Khaalis did not accept the offer, he said he would think about it. With the police commanders in agreement about the severity of the situation at the B'nai B'rith Building, Chief Cullinane was finally moving towards approving Ambassador Zahedi's request, though concern for the ambassadors' safety remained. With Khaalis suspicious the police were preparing an assault to free us, it was going to take all of the ambassadors' negotiating skills for Khaalis to develop a sense of trust and agree to a face-to-face meeting.

CHAPTER THIRTY FIVE

NEGOTIATIONS FOR OUR LIVES

The ambassadors were in contact with Khaalis and were using portions of the Koran to reason with him to have the face-to-face meeting. Ambassador Zahedi again suggested to Khaalis that they meet and for the first time Khaalis moved towards agreement. The police and State Department still opposed the ambassadors going into the building. Ambassador Zahedi told Chief Cullinane he planned on going in and would do so alone if that's what was required. However, agreement on the practical arrangements for the meeting would prove difficult. Cullinane vetoed the ambassadors going to the 8th floor to meet. If any meeting was going to take place, it would be in a part of the building where the police would still have an advantage in case things went badly. It would be up to the ambassadors to convince Khaalis their intentions were pure and they were not part of a plan to trick him and lure him into police hands. The police suggested they meet in the building's lobby. Khaalis was told the participants would be the three ambassadors, Chief Cullinane and Deputy Chief Rabe and Police Commander Joseph O'Brien who had investigated the murder of Khaalis's family and built a relationship with him. Khaalis told the ambassadors that he wanted his son-in-law Azziz to also attend. Then Khaalis insisted that he be allowed to come armed to the meeting with his handguns. Cullinane was insistent that no meeting would take place with Khaalis being armed. The police would not have any weapons and Khaalis could not be carrying a weapon either. Cullinane would insure Khaalis safety during the meeting and he would be allowed to return upstairs afterward. Khaalis was not fully satisfied and became adamant that he be allowed to bring a weapon with him to assure his own safety. After further discussion Chief Cullinane and the ambassadors agreed that Khaalis could bring his long knife. Khaalis finally accepted to the compromise. Now, it was a matter of setting the meeting's time.

While these negotiations were playing out between Khaalis, the ambassadors and police, we had no idea what was going on. After the Feingold incident, it became eerily quiet on the 8th floor. The terrorists were positioned at different points of the floor, each with ammunition bags. Those with carbine rifles had crisscrossed banana clips inserted. We were still lying with our left sides down and right shoulders up. The women were lying flat on the ground as well. Then I noticed that BJ had been brought back into the room. The first time we had seen her since about 2:00 pm on Wednesday. She looked exhausted. Some of the women were talking with her and she shook her head which indicated to me that she didn't know what was happening. I took BJ's reentry as a bad sign. With what we had experienced from early afternoon to this point, along with BJ's re-entry, I was convinced the terrorists thought the police were going to attempt a rescue.

For Ambassador Zahedi, the stage was being set for one of the most important negotiations in his life. He was drawn back to Washington over 30 hours ago because he had this strong feeling deep inside himself that he could help. When he received the call in France, he recalled it was as if God touched his shoulder and helped lead him back to Washington. That's what he had told his King. It is why he pushed his fellow ambassadors, in spite of their concerns, to remain steadfast with him in the quest to save lives.

Ambassador Zahedi also realized the dichotomy he was facing. The siege had evolved to a point of great tension and apprehension. Knowing a rescue attempt would result in the loss of lives, allowed him to finally meet the terrorist leader on a personal basis. He would be able to conduct negotiations face-to-face as he had done his entire diplomatic career. If Khaalis was prepared to surrender or the police felt a rescue attempt could occur without the loss of life among hostages and police officers, the ambassador's good offices and efforts would not have been needed. However, that was not the situation. The face-to-face negotiations would be critical to the outcome.

As part of the preparation, the ambassadors worked with Ambassador Zahedi's aide to find passages in the Koran to use in their discussion with Khaalis. What passage would move Khaalis to show compassion and end the siege? His actions had already killed one, paralyzed another, critically wounded a number of others, severely injured a host of other people as well as physically and emotionally traumatized hundreds. He brought the capital city of our great nation to a standstill. The lives of thousands in Washington had been upended from their daily routines. It was as if the entire city and region were holding their collective breaths hoping and praying for a positive outcome. My colleagues and I didn't know it, but religious institutions throughout the area and across multi denominations were being visited by people who did not know us personally to offer their individual prayers of support for a safe resolution. The same was true in other cities of America as well. Perhaps the prayers and thoughts my colleagues and I were silently saying were being connected to all the prayers of the people on the outside. One could only hope it was true.

The police and FBI were working closely with the ambassadors offering suggestions on how to approach Khaalis and conduct negotiations. Police and FBI psychologists were providing insight as to Khaalis's mental state and his potential reaction to their pleadings and suggestions.

The instructions from Latif and the other terrorists remained clear— we were to remain quiet and there was to be no talking. Even though Khaalis was nearby, we did not know that he also was preparing to meet the ambassadors and the police. Though BJ was close to Khaalis for more than 30 hours, she didn't know his plans. He moved BJ back with us as he did not want her to hear his conversations with the ambassadors and the police about the planned meeting and to know that he was going downstairs. After BJ returned, Latif went over to Khaalis's command area so the two of them could talk. Khaalis was giving specific instructions to Latif that none of the hostages were to be killed while he was downstairs.

Downstairs preparations were being made for a negotiation that had tremendous implications for our lives. The police set up a long table in the lobby of the B'nai B'rith Building with eight chairs. One for Khaalis, three for the ambassadors, plus three for Police Chief Cullinane, Deputy Chief Rabe and Commander O'Brien and one for Khaalis's son-in-law Azziz.

The entourage entered the building about 8:00 pm and waited until Khaalis came downstairs on an elevator.

For Ambassador Zahedi, first impressions were important as he entered a negotiation. He did not know of Khaalis and even though he had been briefed by the police, he was still surprised at the first encounter. When Khaalis arrived, Ambassador Zahedi noted that he was bigger than he thought he would be. Though 56 years of age, Khaalis was in fairly good shape. The ambassador saw that he was stocky and looked strong. He had an ammunition belt around his torso and a large knife that ran through it and attached to his side. The ambassador also thought he looked intimidating and did not seem to be afraid of meeting the police and the ambassadors. He greeted and hugged his son-in-law. He acknowledged Police Chief Cullinane, Deputy Chief Rabe and Commander O'Brien and gave the ambassadors a traditional Islamic greeting. They all sat at the table. The ambassadors' apprehension for their safety and for each of their family's did not abate. Though they were committed to help, they knew they were doing so at considerable risk. They didn't know if the man they were to negotiate with would turn against them. Based on his actions to this point, he didn't seem to care if he and his men gave their lives to his cause. They didn't know if there were explosives in the building and whether Khaalis would be able to signal his men to blow it up.

In the meeting's initial stages, Khaalis was angry and defiant. He covered his demands in great detail. He particularly wanted the killers of his family brought to him for the justice they deserved. He spoke to the ambassadors of his earlier life. He covered his work with the Nation of Islam and how he left that movement due to his differences in their adherence to the Islamic faith. He told them about the formation of the Hanafi movement in Washington and how the Black Muslims had come to his home and killed his family and babies. He said no one would listen to him and now they would need to.

As Khaalis spoke, Ambassador Zahedi wasn't sure how they would get through to him. At times, Khaalis would still question why he should trust them. When he spoke of his demands, Ambassador Zahedi repeated to him that as an ambassador he did not have any sway over the decisions of the police or government. All he had was diplomatic immunity and nothing more. As Khaalis spoke, the ambassadors countered with passages from the Koran, continuing to look for that opening that would allow them to give Khaalis a reason to look for a safe end to the siege. Ambassador Zahedi thought of his critical tango analogy that he would use in his negotiations. At this moment, he wasn't sure if he had a person who wanted to tango. The ambassador thought the acts that Khaalis had initiated were reprehensible, but at the same time he felt sad about the tragic killing of his family. As he listened to Khaalis review his demands, always going back to his family, the ambassador started to wonder, was the connection to his family the road to a basis for negotiation.

Over the course of his diplomatic career Ambassador Zahedi had engaged in negotiations with world leaders. He had been part of the deliberations that focused on peace such as the Israeli Arab conflict, on regional tensions between Pakistan and India and among the neighbors of Iran such as the Soviet Union where centuries of mistrust still existed. He considered the elements of those discussions and what led to success or failure. He knew that the same skills he utilized in those negotiations were going to be required in these delicate conversations with a man who held many people's lives in his hands. He also thought about aspects of his own life and how they might be helpful in bringing the crisis to a successful conclusion.

The ambassador was still taken aback from what he encountered upon his return to Washington from Nice. He had never seen the city in such a state of siege. He knew how serious the circumstances were based on the police description of a potential rescue attempt and the eventual loss of lives from that plan. Now he was sitting across from a man who, he was convinced, would give up his own life and also kill his hostages. The ambassador again thought of his grandmother and remembered how shocked he was when she died. He visualized the first time he saw his father after he had been imprisoned for three years and how shocked he was seeing how he looked. Now, he was feeling that same level of shock that he felt during a number of personal situations in his life. It was these feelings that led him to try and speak to Khaalis in very personal terms.

While the face-to-face negotiations were proceeding downstairs, we were still lying in our protective position—keep your left side and head down. It had been six hours and the only positive thoughts that I could find were that if the shooting began, some divine intervention would occur and I would survive the ordeal. It wasn't that I was wishing bad things for my colleagues. I was finding hope and strength in locking in on a thought that it would not be me. It might not have been a very rational thought but for me it was tied into my strong desire to survive. I don't know what my colleagues were thinking at that very moment but I would have to believe were the same.

My position allowed me to swivel my head from time-to-time and look across and see numerous colleagues. The fear and exhaustion on people's faces were evident. On the far right hand side was Steve Morrison, next to him was Joe Sklover who in spite of his heart condition was holding up fairly well, next was Sid Closter, near Sid was Horace Gold. I thought I had heard at one time that Horace wore a colostomy bag and I wondered how he was doing at this stage. Gerd Strauss, the volunteer leader stuck in the building was near Horace. Immediately next to them were Norman Buckner, Jerry Rudman and Jay Manchester, David Brody and Bernie Simon. On my other side were Dale Bell and a man named Meridith who worked for B'nai B'rith Women. In front of me was David Royal a young man from our mail room. He had donated a kidney to his mother a short time ago. Also near were Mike Brice from the mail room, Bill Korey, David Leshnick and next to him was a young man from the fund raising office who had just started, I did not know his name though I think he was an Israeli. Going down the line there was Bill Ferguson from the computer room. On the other side of Bill was Danny the Carpenter as we called him as well as another painter who I did not know by name. I looked over at Stanley Cahn who was in the fund raising department and lying in that area. I was transfixed at what I saw. Stan looked physically different. I thought my eyes were playing tricks on me, but that was not the case. He did look different. Stan was stoutly built, always seemed to have a five o'clock shadow and was a person who seemed angry at times. I was now looking at a person whose face lines had changed. He had a softer look about him and for the first time that I had known him, I saw how blue his eyes were. He had physically changed. I didn't know it at the time, but the women across from the men were having these exact conversations among themselves. They were watching the men change physically in front of their eyes. Near Stan was Norman Frimmer, a Rabbi who was the head of the Hillel college program. The row continued with Charlie Fenyevesi and Dick Greenwood from the insurance program who worked for Lawrie Kaplan. Dick obviously did not make it into Lawrie's office where others had barricaded themselves early on Wednesday. Dick was a nice man, who like Sid Clearfield, was never without a cigarette when I saw him. He and Sid must have been having nicotine fits by this time. The line of colleagues in my sight also included Sid Clearfield, Lew Hamburger, Rabbi Sam Fishman and Si Cohen. Near Si were a number of painters whose names I did not know. Dick Burg, from the Israel Commission to whom Marilyn Bargteil had apologized profusely for having to lie on top of him in the beginning of the siege was also nearby.

Looking at my colleagues, knowing some better than others, I recognized that each person on the 8th floor had a name and a personal story. They had family, friends and acquaintances thinking about them. I'm sure they were concerned for their lives and at the same time were hopeful they would see them again. Though the terrorists had controlled our lives for more than 30 hours, they did not control our dignity, our ability to show compassion to others, in spite of a grievous situation, and our will to survive. We continued to find strength and comfort from each other in a very real life and death situation.

Downstairs, Ambassador Zahedi thought to himself that he had finally found in the recess of his experiences a story that could prove to be beneficial in reaching a successful outcome to the hostage crisis. He told Khaalis that he would like to relay to him a personal story he had heard many times from his grandmother that he felt had similarities to Khaalis's own situation. His Grandfather was a leader in the tribal area where they lived when his father was 9 or 10 years old. At times, the tribal disagreements led to armed conflict. His grandfather went on a mission to bring peace among the tribes. He arrived at the enemy tribe and was on horseback sharing a water pipe with his adversaries. As he spoke with enemy leaders, suddenly a number of the enemy tribe's men shot at him. One of the bullets struck his heart and killed him. The conflict continued and year's later men from his grandfather's tribe captured the men who had killed his grandfather. They brought them back to their area so his grandmother could see the killers before they were executed. His grandmother came out of her dwelling to see them. As she looked at them she told them that in her heart she had forgiven them for the deed they had done and that she was not going to let the men of her tribe kill them. She wanted to spare their lives. As Ambassador Zahedi finished his story there was total silence among those sitting around the table. The ambassador followed up his story by saying to Khaalis that he needed to show the same compassion to his hostages that his grandmother had shown the killers of his grandfather.

Khaalis had been listening intently to the ambassador and had continuous eye contact with him as he related this very personal experience. Shortly after Ambassador Zahedi had finished, Khaalis made a quick motion and jumped to his feet which startled everyone sitting around the table. As Khaalis made his way towards Ambassador Zahedi, the ambassador also rose and wasn't sure what was going to happen. Khaalis got to him and hugged him with tears in his eyes. He told Ambassador Zahedi that he trusted him and that he believed he was a person with whom he could do business. Finally, Ambassador Zahedi had a person who would tango.

Khaalis returned to his seat. Ambassador Zahedi and the other ambassadors felt they were making progress. They suggested to Khaalis that he release a number of hostages in a show of good faith. They further suggested that releasing up to 30 hostages would be a very strong indication that a peaceful solution could be worked out. Khaalis remained silent for some time and then he uttered some words that caught the ambassadors, Cullinane and Rabe off guard. He said, "Why don't I release all of them?" There was stunned silence and a deep feeling of relief coming over the people who were negotiating for our lives. As they took in Khaalis's words, he followed up with his demands. As they heard them, they realized they might be a sticking point and envisioned a problem implementing the deal Khaalis was suggesting. He told them that he couldn't be treated like the murderers of his family and sent to jail like them. He wanted to be treated with the dignity that he felt he deserved and to go home and be with his family. Ambassador Zahedi once again emphasized to Khaalis that such decisions were out of his control and were in the hands of the authorities. The ambassador did not want the trust they had worked so hard to build to quickly dissipate. It was now Police Chief Cullinane and Deputy Chief Rabe's turn to engage in the negotiations. The told Khaalis they would need to make some calls to see if they could make the arrangements Khaalis suggested. They alone could not make the deal happen and it was going to take a coordinated effort among the police, FBI, Justice Department and District Court to work through the issue. Khaalis and his men had managed to violate numerous federal criminal statues and officials were not inclined to just give him a pass. The terrorist activity and hate crimes that he and his men had carried out had killed one and injured many. He had crippled the nation's capital for 40 hours. Throughout the entire siege, Cullinane had kept Griffin Bell, the Attorney General of the United States and FBI Director Clarence Kelly briefed. Nick Stames, head of the FBI's Washington office and Patrick Mullany the FBI's premier hostage and terrorism expert were also involved from the very beginning.

Cullinane reached out to the Justice Department and Attorney General Bell and Superior Court officials who would be involved in any jurisdiction decisions. Judge Harold Greene, who would need to approve any agreement, was initially hesitant in sanctioning a plan to let free any of the terrorists on their own personal recognizance. Chief Cullinane was convinced that for a successful conclusion, it was essential that Khaalis's demand allowing him to go home would be met. The ability to go home did not apply to all of his followers except those at the Islamic Center. Since they had not utilized a gun in the commitment of the crime, the District of Columbia's liberal arrest statues allowed those terrorists to go home as well. The other terrorists from the B'nai B'rith Building and District Building were to be arrested and held.

The tense situation on the 8th floor remained. We had no idea that Khaalis has slipped downstairs. The terrorists around the room were vigilant and on edge. During this time period a middle aged black woman who I did not know become hysterical. She seemed on the verge of a nervous breakdown and was now the second person after Norman Feingold to manifest in a physical and vocal way the toll the siege was having on people. A number of women were trying unsuccessfully to console her. Latif, on the other side of the floor, heard the commotion and came back. He moved toward the woman as her wails grew and told her to be quiet, but she wasn't responding positively. Then he told the women around her that they needed to quiet her down and that it would all be over soon. My famously well know optimistic side grabbed onto that statement and I focused on us getting out. At the same time, my other senses were certainly delivering an opposite message with the prospect that many of us might be killed shortly.

Though not a highly religious person in terms of following the daily strictures of the Orthodox, I do have a strong belief in a God. For a number of hours that Thursday evening I was having a personal conversation with

God in a manner that I had never experienced before. What was going to happen to me–to us–was out of our individual control. Being tied up hand and foot added to this helpless feeling. As I struggled with my emotions, I could not comprehend that I wasn't going to see Jane and Emily again.

At about this time, Latif loudly called out that our TV man was coming back and I heard the elevator operating. I was totally perplexed at what Latif said. Were they were allowing a TV camera crew to come up to the 8th floor and film us? I just couldn't believe it. I could hear warm greetings being exchanged and I fully expected to see a camera crew appear from around the corner near the elevator bank and start to film us. When that did not occur, I wasn't sure what was happening. Latif had not re-appeared in our area and I did not realize that he was being briefed by Khaalis on his own fate and the fate of his fellow terrorists. Khaalis was going home and Latif and the others were heading to jail.

CHAPTER THIRTY SIX

THE END AND DEALING WITH THE AFTERMATH

Sometime later Latif came into the room and seemed a bit disoriented. He said, "I'm sorry we didn't get a chance to feed you." He let a number of women distribute food to the other women. Soon afterward he let a number of women begin to distribute food to the men and help them eat and drink since our hands and feet remained tied. The women left a sandwich and can of soda near each of us and then started on the far side away from where I was situated to help men eat. I was looking at my sandwich and can of coke thinking I'm sure they will taste good. I was just going to have to wait my turn. The mood of the gunmen had noticeably changed. We were allowed to talk at higher decibel levels then at the start of the siege. The mood among my fellow captives was also more jovial and our spirits had lifted up some from the incredible tension we were feeling just a short time ago. Latif was standing near me and since the mood had changed I thought I would try to have a brief conversation with him and make a request. I asked if he would tie my hands in front of me so I could feed myself. He thought about my request for a moment and then he came over to me, untied my hands and retied my hands in front. I thanked him and he backed away to continue observing what was happening among the hostages. Though the two Daytril I was given earlier offered some brief relief from the pain in my shoulders, the discomfort levels had soon returned and having my hands tied to the front was a wonderful relief. I would have gladly taken that gesture even without food, though I didn't waste much time starting to eat the sandwich and drink the Coke. Making the best out of the situation, I pretended I was at a picnic. The sandwich tasted good and that Coke tasted even better. Though not a conscious thought at the time, based on the previous experience concerning food I'm sure many of us wondered when we might eat again. When we finished we were instructed to calm down and stop talking. The picnic atmosphere disappeared quickly and everyone was told to settle down for the evening and go to sleep. For the first time during the siege, they adjusted the lights and made it darker in the room. Everyone was settling in for the night. We were a little calmer after having some food but still expecting the ordeal to continue. The physiological aspect of eating made it easier to close my eyes and try to get some sleep. The hardness of the floor had not changed and it was colder in the room than the previous evening so even though I was trying to force myself to fall asleep, it just wasn't happening.

When I opened my eyes, the first thing I noticed not seeing was the gunman who always sat on the right hand side of the room. He had disappeared, and that helped to raise my apprehension levels. My immediate thought was that the SWAT team was coming up in the elevators or the stairwell and they were directing their fire power at these locations. The food and more jovial mood we had been feeling was once again a prelude and a terrible jolt back to the reality of our situation and the consequences that were always hiding below the surface. We heard the elevators start to work and then the doors open. Then, a single man dressed in blue with a helmet and face shield and what looked like an M16 rifle quickly came into the room. He rushed to the center between the men and women and went to one knee. He had his gun in front of him and was aiming it from side-to-side covering the area where we were located. Two other men came running into the room and proceeded to the darkened area of the 8th floor where the terrorist had accidently discharged his weapon early Thursday morning. They took up positions there. Then they started yelling at the top of their voices, some of it obscenity laced, that they were Police SWAT and they wanted everyone to remain down, keep their heads down and be quiet. No one moved–everyone was frozen. While they were barking orders, fear and apprehension had reached new levels among the hostages. Were the SWAT team members positioning themselves for a firefight with the terrorists? One of the hostages disobeyed the police orders and yelled out to thank God. They just couldn't contain themselves. Other people around the room started to cry. Within moments, everyone started to talk at once. The SWAT team members continued to scream at us to remain quiet, stay calm and keep down. I guess they didn't realize what a difficult task it would be in keeping a room filled with so many Jews quiet. I noticed off to my right, on the dark side of the room, I saw Police Chief Cullinane. I recognized him from a picture I had seen. He was near the door where one of the gunmen had taken his nap and the door was closed. One of the SWAT team members tried to open the door but it was locked and he quickly pulled up his rifle in front of him. Another SWAT team member grabbed one of Cullinane's arms and pulled him out of the way. The chief looked startled by the action. Not knowing what might be in the room, the one who was in front of the door reacted quickly and kicked the door open. There was a great deal of screaming as he went in and was joined by others. They saw the room was empty. There were a number of SWAT team members throughout the 8th floor. I'm sure there were more than I realized since there must have been SWAT team members on the other side of the 8th floor where Khaalis has set up his own command center. Though they had been in the room about five minutes, they made no effort to untie us. I was lying over on the left side of where we were being held and standing above me was a SWAT team member. He called over a colleague, who appeared to be the person in charge, to have a discussion. He was pointing to where I was lying and I knew exactly what they were discussing and was becoming disturbed. As the terrorists rotated us around the side of the room where the men were tied up, by Thursday afternoon I was now near a majority of the young men that worked in our mail room. The majority of them were black. The two police officers were now pointing at my black colleagues. I looked at the two officers and told them they were with us and I didn't hide my annoyance. I kept repeating myself, they are with us. The officer in charge finally came over to me and asked that I look at the young men lying around me and could I identify them. I looked around and said yes and he obviously didn't take my word. He then asked me to personally name each of them which I did. The officer in charge then looked from one side of the room to the other and asked in a loud voice, "Can everyone vouch for everyone in this room?" And everyone responded, "Yes." Finally, people were allowed to untie each other and greet each other. People who were never close and never said hello in the building before, were saying hello and kissing and hugging one another. Men and women met in the center of the room and the police SWAT team were intermingled among us. Norman Frimmer, recited the Shechionu, the Hebrew prayer thanking God for allowing one to reach a new season. There was euphoria in the room. The ending happened so quickly, that at first it was hard to comprehend it was actually over. I walked over to Madelyn Herman who was crying and hugged her and told her everything was ok. I sought out David Leshnick and we hugged and I kidded him that I told him I knew that we'd get out. The police were trying to sort things out and gain some control over the situation as emotions among us were running high. They had determined they would evacuate the injured first. One of officers looked at me and he grabbed my arm and said to come with him and he led me towards the elevator away from the vast majority of my colleagues. They loaded a number of us on the elevator and as I got out on the lobby floor Bernie Sullivan, the chief building engineer was standing near the door that led to the alley. He had a huge grin on his face. I shook Bernie's hand and quickly realized he probably had not yet seen his daughter who was one of the hostages. The door to the alley was open and as I stepped through, there was a corridor of police SWAT team members all armed and in full battle gear standing shoulder to shoulder. They had formed a pathway that went from the B'nai B'rith Building to a door leading to the Gramercy Inn. As I walked between the lines of police SWAT, they had smiles on their faces and a number of them shook my hand or patted me on the back. Afterwards, I'm not sure I thanked them as I walked over to the hotel. I should have been thanking them profusely. As I looked at their faces and saw their smiles and nods of encouragement, I realized that some of these men might have had to sacrifice their own lives to save us. They were a happy group of people who I am sure would have carried out their responsibilities no matter the personal danger they might have faced. Based on their demeanor, there was no question they were happy at the negotiated outcome.

Standing quietly off to the side of the SWAT corridor, between the two buildings, was Patrick Mullany. He was watching as we left the B'nai B'rith Building. He was emotionally and physically tired and I didn't realize it at the time, but I walked right by him. As he watched us go by, he had felt a tremendous relief the ordeal was over. As he participated in the negotiations, he wasn't fully convinced that he would see us leave the building alive. He knew that he had been part of an unprecedented effort of cooperation between agencies that at times were wary of one another. The cooperation between the District Police, FBI, Justice Department, State Department, White House and others was a major factor in the successful conclusion he was now witnessing. Throw in the international aspect of three Arab ambassadors being engaged and the confluence of all these elements coming together had never occurred before. He truly felt a personal and professional satisfaction that in some way he was part of the effort that saved our lives.

As I stepped into the Gramercy, there was a hotel staff member with a tray of poured bourbon ready to be consumed. Never being a drinker I declined and asked for some Coke which they had on another tray. I noticed that Norman Buckner was right behind me, he grabbed one of the glasses and consumed it in one big swallow. He looked satisfied and I thought maybe I should relent and become a drinker right there on the spot. Then Charlie Fishman greeted me. A colleague, he was sitting at a table with a list of names and checking us off as we entered. Charlie got up and we hugged each other across the table. I found out afterward that his job during the ordeal was to help the management and police try and figure out who was in the building. Jane told me afterwards that Charlie had called to check on my whereabouts that Wednesday. I asked Charlie how I could reach Janie and he said he was making the calls and not to worry. I finally looked to my left and Norman and I looked at each other for a few seconds and he reached across, gave me a short hug and kissed me on the cheek. I then noticed the man who was standing in front of me on the 3rd floor landing. We finally had a chance to introduce ourselves and he told me he was Jay Nichols. We smiled and shook hands. He looked at me and said "You know, you look just like Joe Namath after a bad game." I told him I'd heard that comparison before. I asked him if he was alright and he said he would be okay. From behind I felt a hand take my arm and I saw it was a policeman who brought me over to another table next to where Charlie was sitting. There was a police officer with a pad and he asked me my name, home address and telephone number. He asked how I was injured and I told him I had been hit in the face with a rifle. He then passed me off to an officer next to him who took a few pictures of me with his camera. I quickly determined I had just become evidence.

There were a few other colleagues in the room. I saw Faye Hoffman with whom I had started my Wednesday morning off with coffee in her office. Having not seen Faye the entire time, I knew she wasn't one of the hostages but did not know how she had escaped the ordeal. We gave each other a hug and she asked if I was ok. However, it was apparent that she was focused on the person behind me–Norman. I felt it was more than just a casual interest in a co-worker. Here I was–just released from a life and death situation–picking up vibes about two colleagues. How interesting the human experience is. The hostage siege had a tremendous impact on the individuals who were involved, both physically and emotionally. The ramifications of surviving the event for many would be life altering. It became obvious from almost the moment we were released that many of them thought about what they would do differently with their lives if they had a second chance. Perhaps their wishes and fantasies would never manifest themselves into a reality if their lives went along their normal daily path. The terrorist siege for some became an electric volt that awakened their need to do what they were thinking about up on the 8th floor. Secrets that had been kept, some better than others, emerged. At 2:00 am on Friday, March 11th, literally minutes after we were released, I knew that Norman Buckner and Faye Hoffman had a relationship that was beyond being colleagues and perhaps they didn't care that others would know even though Norman's wife and family most likely were waiting to greet him. Sometime later, Norman divorced his wife Jeanne and he and Faye were married. There were others who had relationships with work colleagues that became known and life altering choices were made. For some it wasn't the influence of another person, but the processing of thoughts over a 40-hour period of tremendous strain, self-examination and promises to oneself that caused marriages to dissolve, a desire for changes in life style and career.

As the police officer finished taking my picture, I moved towards the hotel lobby and was enjoying my glass of Coke– it was one of the best I had ever had. Another officer approached and told me there were buses in front of the hotel to take the injured to the hospital. At that point the euphoria of being free had taken over. I didn't feel tired and was not concentrating on my injury. I told him that I didn't think I needed to go to the hospital. He looked at my face and my clothes that were still covered with blood and disagreed. His tone told me that it was not my decision. He walked me out to the bus and I was one of the first to board. In the early morning chill, just wearing my dress shirt and slacks, I thought it would be nice to have my suit coat and then remembered it was hanging over the back of a chair in my office on the 5th floor. The chances of getting it were not very good. I began to notice a few other things that had happened in the last moments being on the 8th floor that must have been reactions without thought. When I was finally untied by the police, I placed my tie in my right front pants pocket and I felt it there. My Seiko watch with the blue face that Jane had given me in June of 1971, which Latif had removed on Thursday, was still in my left front pants pocket. I just left it there. I had worn that watch every day for the last six years. I also felt for my wallet and remembered I didn't have it. Latif had removed it and put it in the bucket with the other wallets when he wanted us to experience being frisked. I walked with the officer toward the bus which was pointed north on Rhode Island Avenue.

As I walked to the bus, there was a sound in the air that that seemed to be coming from different directions. It was church bells. Churches throughout the Washington area started to ring their bells at the announcement of our release. Shortly after 2:00 am on Friday, March 11th, Washington was celebrating. It was an incredible feeling to hear the bells tolling.

I walked onto the bus and the only person on was the driver who shook my hand and smiled. The police officer also followed me on. I looked out the back window of the bus towards Scott Circle and I noticed that police barricades had been set up blocking traffic from entering Rhode Island Avenue. As I looked out there were crowds of people standing behind the barricades in the middle of the circle and back where Massachusetts Avenue started. I walked to the back of the bus for a better look and the people at the circle noticed me and started to clap and wave their hands. Some had taken off their hats and were waving them at me as well. I waved back and did so for several minutes. I asked the officer if the people out there were curiosity seekers. He said no, that people had gathered there for almost the entire 40 hours expressing concern and hope. He was sure that many came out after they heard we were released and that the ringing of the church bells throughout the city was bringing people out as well. I turned back to the window and waved again. A few of my colleagues finally joined me on the bus, one being Jerry Rudman who had also been injured by a rifle butt just above his eyebrow. They decided to take us to George Washington University Hospital which is located on Washington Circle. The streets were deserted and the ride up M Street and over to K Street was quick. The bus parked in front of the hospital's emergency room door which looked out on Washington Circle.

On a nice day in Washington, you'd find students and those who worked in the area sitting on the park benches that surround the circle. As I got off the bus, I saw a solitary figure standing on the curb of the circle. It was an associate, Mort Feigenbaum. His wife Shirley had been a hostage and I didn't know whether he had seen her yet. Mort saw me about the same time and I walked across the street towards him and we met in the middle. As he came up to me Mort started to cry and he hugged me and held me for a few minutes. Looking at my face he asked if I was ok and he kissed me on the cheek. I told him Shirley was ok. He seemed incredibly distraught and I told him everything was ok. He said I should go in and get myself checked out. As I left, looking back, Mort was still standing in the middle of the street crying.

There were two nurses standing at the door when I entered the hospital. One had a tray with about a 100 hypodermic needles that she was holding with both hands. The other nurse asked me what happened and I told her I had been hit in the face with a rifle barrel. As I told her this, she undid the button on my long sleeve shirt, rolled up the sleeve, quickly swabbed my arm with some alcohol and hit me with one of the needles. I said, "Nice to meet you too" and what was that. She told me I would probably have no problem remembering when I got my last tetanus shot, which she just gave me. She truly was a clairvoyant who looked into the future for that shot became ingrained in my memory.

Another nurse took me to an examining room across the center of the emergency room. We passed a long hallway that served as a spoke leading to the emergency room. I glanced to my right and stopped. The hallway probably was at least a 100 feet long. From the top of the hallway, all the way down as far as I could see, there were hospital gurneys along both sides of the wall with a narrow path between them. Each gurney had a long pole connected to it and some kind of intravenous bag attached to the pole.

The nurse leading the way was now standing next to my shoulder and we were looking down the hallway. I said to her they obviously were expecting something different then what they were experiencing. She told me they were instructed to prepare for the worst—many injured with the potential of a large number of gunshot wounds and life threatening injuries among the hostages.

We were both very quiet and she could sense that what I was seeing was disturbing and sobering. The picture of the hallway was now placed into my memory bank and a small part of the euphoria I was experiencing had been deflated a bit. The reality of how bad it was, and how bad it could have been, confirmed many of my thoughts while I was lying on the 8th floor. It truly started to sink in that perhaps I might not have seen Jane and Emily and enjoyed that Mr. Goodbar.

The nurse gently took my hand and led me towards the examining room. The adrenaline that took over when we were released had masked the pain in my face and any potential serious harm.

A few emergency room doctors came in to examine me. They wanted to take some x-rays to get a better sense of what had happened. They sent me upstairs to radiology where a technician was waiting. He told me to lie on the table and started to put me in uncomfortable positions. One he had me do you learn in football practice–a bridge. You basically lift your butt up from the ground and place your weight on your neck and you are now looking behind you and you can rock back and forth. He had me do this to get a good picture of the injured area.

Those who know me would tell you that I always prided myself on my manners and how I treated people. As I was in this position, I stared cursing at the technician and asked whether he was related to the terrorists.

It should have been the first indication to me that I was beginning to experience the impact of how we were treated and spoken to for 40 hours. I didn't realize that I was interspersing curse words in every conversation I was having with people.

When we arrived at Ft. Lauderdale airport a number of days after being released, it wasn't until I was in the car with my mother and brother Barry that this was apparent to everyone but me. Barry asked Jane if I was okay since during the ride from the airport to my in-laws apartment I was cursing like a trucker, which surprised them. Barry finally pointed it out to me and I began to think about what I was saying and readjust my language.

I imagine the technician was glad to send me back downstairs to the emergency room doctors. By the time I arrived, a plastic surgeon and ophthalmologist had joined them. They were all looking at my x-ray and told me the injury was worse than they originally thought.

The rifle barrel had crushed my zygomatic bone and broke my cheekbone in six places from the bridge of my nose to my earlobe. They wanted me to see their colleague, Paul Zamick, on Monday to get his opinion on treatment options. Since I had not received treatment for 40 hours they were going to leave it alone. They further cleaned my wound, put a bandage on it and released me.

By this time it was close to 4:30 am and I had not spoken with Janie. I wasn't sure where she was and did not know if she knew where I was. One of the nurses told me the staging area for families was the Foundry Methodist Church at P and 16th Streets not far from the B'nai B'rith Building. I asked if they had the phone number and could I use a phone. The receptionist handed me a phone and found the number.

I called and explained who I was and could they locate Jane Green. They told me to hold on and I could hear a large amount of background noise. Finally, Janie came on the line and I told her that I had been injured, but okay. She said she got to the church and couldn't find me with the others. Someone finally told her that I had been injured and taken to George Washington Hospital. She was with Paula Rudman who had been told about Jerry at the same time. I asked her to tell Paula that I was with Jerry, that he was okay, and we were both heading to the church shortly.

When I was finally checked out, there were just a few of us left at the hospital and all the buses had been dispersed. Someone from the hospital told us he was going to get us a ride and a few minutes later they brought up a medical vehicle that looked like a station wagon.

All the way in back was a bench seat facing backwards and a rear door that opened sideways. It reminded me of a station wagon my father owned back in the late '50'-s and being the youngest of four, I was relegated to that back seat and riding backwards. I immediately headed to the back to assume the seating position that I had done for numerous years. Ralph

184

Basillio joined me. As we waited for the driver, a photographer ran up to the back and took our picture.

The streets of Washington remained empty and quiet and the ride to the church was quick. As we pulled up to the side entry I hopped out of the back with Ralph and the first person I saw was Dan Thursz standing out near the street. He met me half way and gave me a big hug. At 6'7", I came up to Dan's chest. He asked me if I was okay.

Leaving Dan I finally saw Janie and we hugged and gave each other a kiss. I think my call that I was ok made her feel better. I asked her if she had a Mr. Goodbar with her and she had a quizzical look on her face–I told her I'd tell her later. Right behind Janie was her close friend from New Jersey Vicki Franklin whom I was surprised to see. Vicki had come to stay with Janie and she came over and held on to me for awhile.

Paula Rudman, who I had met casually in the past, came up and gave me a hug and a kiss on the cheek. We headed towards the door and when we entered I didn't realize what we had stepped into. It was mayhem as I came through the door. Reporters and photographers rushed forward shouting questions and flash bulbs were going off.

I was stunned and couldn't work my way through the crowd. Paula grabbed my hand to try and lead me. Harvey Berk from the B'nai B'rith Youth Organization was a big guy and he started to push people out of the way, yelling at them to leave me alone. They ushered me towards an area of the church that had been walled off by a curtain. Behind the curtain was a table set up with food and drinks and some chairs where only the hostages, family members and B'nai B'rith colleagues could enter.

It was quieter in the back, though you could hear the substantial noise out front. I grabbed a soda and it seemed that things were happening at a frenetic pace. I was trying to answer everyone's questions and get a sense of my surroundings. It was then that I realized that I was really tired and asked if I had to do anything else there or could we head home. To avoid the crowd out front, we left by a side door. Janie and Vicki walked me to the car. Jane said she hoped they hadn't towed it since she left it in a tow away zone. The car was a few blocks away and when we saw it she said to Vicki their sign had worked. They left a note on the front dash board that said—Do Not Tow, Hostage at B'nai B'rith Building. Thirty-four years later, I still have that note.

They had me lie down on the back seat; the two of them, though exhausted themselves, were hyper. They were talking quickly, trying to fill me in on what was happening on the outside. Janie said family members from both sides were calling incessantly and they all wanted to come up and be with her and she didn't want any of them. When Vicki called insisting that she come, the discussion from Florida ended.

Our neighbor Ann Gallagher was at the apartment with Emily and our dog Maudie. We got home, went up in the elevator and walked down the long hallway and Janie opened the door. Ann met us and she hugged me for a long time. Maudie started barking and became excited to see me. Emily was sleeping in her room and we were all trying not to wake her. I walked by her room, and as if she had a sense about something being amiss, she jumped up in her crib and I went to get her.

The phone, which Jane told me had never stopped during the entire ordeal, was already ringing at 5:30 am–family members and some colleagues who had avoided capture.

Jane made me some breakfast and since I couldn't shower, I decided on a bath. As I waited for Jane to run the bath I sat there and took stock of my physical well being. My face hurt, my shoulders hurt and I thought that the vast majority of the bones in my body hurt as well. I wondered, is this how an old man would feel and if so, I felt very old.

When I made it into the bath its warmth was one of the nicest feelings ever. Jane continued to answer the phone as I soaked and I fell asleep. Not hearing anything from the bathroom she and Vicki became concerned and came to check on me. Afraid I was going to slip down and drown myself they woke me up. They got me out of the tub and into bed where I fell into a deep sleep. It was total exhaustion. In the immediate hours after the siege, I had no dreams. I was just too exhausted to dream. They would come later.

Occasionally I would hear the phone ring and Jane speaking with someone. After one call she came into to see if I was awake and would I take a call. There were two colleagues on the line from Chicago begging her to get me on the phone. She came and gently woke me to take the call since they said they would continue to call every few minutes to see if I was awake.

It was Rabbi Oscar Groner, Assistant National Director of Hillel and Rabbi Joel Pupko, Hillel Rabbi at the University of Michigan in Ann

Arbor and now running a regional program in Chicago. Both were more than colleagues, they had become friends.

The best way to describe our conversation was they were crazed–upset, concerned, angry with a host of emotions rushing out during the call. I spoke with them for awhile and gave them a brief review of what we experienced. They said they had spoken with a number of colleagues and that I seemed to be the only one who could have a rational conversation with them. As I spoke with them, I realized that they were just as traumatized as I was, though in a different way. They felt a bit ashamed they were not with us in the building. From my standpoint they weren't missing anything, but the feelings of guilt they were experiencing was evident. They were not alone in those feelings among others who by happen chance were out of the building or out of town and those feelings would last for some time.

A call came on Sunday morning from George Spectre who had warned management repeatedly about the lack of security and the dangers lurking, all to no avail. George called early Sunday and said he wanted to come over to visit though he lived in Virginia. Janie told him I was still sleeping more than awake and a visit at this time probably wasn't a good idea. George told her it would take him about 45 minutes to get to White Oak and he was on his way whether we wanted him or not.

George arrived and came into the bedroom to sit with me. He shook my hand and sat in a chair across from the bed. Almost immediately he started to cry. He was angry and talking about how they wouldn't listen to him and now look what had occurred. I could tell that he was upset that he was not in the building and was troubled that he wasn't more persuasive with management.

The pattern among colleagues, those who were not part of the hostage group, was becoming evident. A day later, it also became clear that there was another group of colleagues in the building who had not been captured.

On the Monday following the terrorist siege, I had an appointment with the plastic surgeon about my injury. The following day, Jane, Emily and I were flying to Florida to be with family and for me to begin the recovery process. Steve Widdes and Anna Cohn offered to take me to the appointment and I asked that we stop by the building so I could go in before leaving town. We headed there after the doctor's appointment. Entering, we encountered an armed security guard who was posted near the elevators.

We had to sign in and show identification. I told him I didn't have any since my wallet had been taken. Steve and Anna vouched for me.

I first went to the 5th floor where my office was located. Coming off the elevator, I ran into Norma Klein, Harold Brenner's assistant who had been barracaded with Harold and Lawrie at the beginning of the siege. She started to cry and held on to me for a long time. She kept saying, look what they've done to you. Next, Harold came over, kissed me on the cheek and started to cry. He was extremely upset and I was trying to calm his emotions.

There were a few other people on the floor and it seemed they were trying to bring back some normalcy but were having difficulty doing so. We chatted for a few minutes and then I started to walk around the building and take in what we experienced. I looked in the stairwells and saw they were still stuffed with office equipment. The inevitable clean up had not started.

We went up to the 8th floor and I had a chance to just stand in the middle of the floor and bring back images that would be with me the remainder of my life. I finally had a chance to see where Khaalis set up his office outside of David Brody's office and where BJ served as his secretary for almost 36 hours. I walked back to the room where they stored their array of weapons and stopped short when I saw the hole in the wall that occurred when the 357 magnum had discharged in the early morning hours of March 10th. The size of the hole was impressive and also sobering.

I looked down both stairwells, saw the destruction, and knew it would take some time to clear it all out.

I went to the 7th floor to let Dan Thurz know I'd be leaving town. I was not going to ask permission; it was a discussion to inform. When I got to his office it looked disheveled, numerous items were broken and things were out of place.

There were a few colleagues around the area and as I turned the corner to Dan's office, I saw him seated at his desk and speaking with Si Cohen. Si was telling Dan that he needed some time to off to process what he just went through and work on his physical and mental well being. Dan told Si that he expected him back at work at his desk the next day. Si got up and we nodded at one another. He looked terrible. We asked each other how we were doing, shook hands and he patted me on the back.

Dan saw me and waved me in and pointed towards a chair. After what I just witnessed I thought this should be an interesting conversation. I had another feeling—he truly did not comprehend or understand what his staff had just experienced. For a guy with a doctorate in social work, I expected more empathy. He asked how I was doing and I told him that I'd be taking some time off; I wasn't sure how long, but I'd be back. He told me to take all the time I needed and not to worry. Obviously a consistent approach to employee requests was not being applied. I felt bad for Si and hoped that he'd take the time he needed anyway.

When I came back after 10 days, and actually was with Dan for a fund raising breakfast in Florida, there were messages from the police that I was needed for an interview. They had set up an area in the building. Since I had been injured, it was decided that I would be called as a witness. It took an entire afternoon to give my statement to a police detective. He told me that I would be hearing from the U.S. Attorney's office to set up another meeting and yes, I'd be testifying in the trial.

One of the things I also needed to do with the police was to recover my wallet. The detective told me who to call and I located the people in charge of evidence at police headquarters. There I was exposed to a side of society with which I did not have much experience. People in handcuffs were being escorted around the building, there was coarseness and feeling of menace that permeated the building along with what seemed a constant loud noise. I had never been the victim of a crime of violence and it had changed my life. The office was on an upper floor and I had to wait to fill out forms to get my wallet. I couldn't get out of that headquarters building fast enough. Perhaps I didn't realize it at the time, but some form of post traumatic stress was evident though I had convinced myself that I was functioning normally and was getting on with my life.

CHAPTER THIRTY SEVEN

THE TRIAL

A short time later, I received a call from the U.S. Attorney's office to set up an appointment. I went to their offices where I met Mark Touhey and Martin Linsky, two young attorneys who had drawn the assignment of prosecuting the case. We went over my statement and they walked me through what would happen when I finally showed up to testify. They also covered what would happen during jury selection and what to expect. They were particularly interested in that part of my statement when Abdul Adam had the radio on. That's when I heard about the other buildings and Khaalis came out to exclaim his men had succeeded in their endeavor. They thought this helped buttress the felony murder count the terrorists faced in addition to kidnapping and a variety of assault charges. As I understood the law, felony murder is where you try to tie someone to a murder even though they were not present when it occurred. Maurice Williams was killed at the District Building and they wanted to prove that Khaalis and his men at our building and the mosque were just as guilty of that murder. Attorney friends also told me that charge is very hard to prove to a jury. I told Mark and Martin that even though I heard and saw what happened, it was one of the more murky points of the ordeal. They told me not to worry, they wouldn't bring it up. I discovered that I had been a way too trusting person when it came to playing in this new arena.

The trial was assigned to Nicholas Nunzio a respected District Superior Court Judge who had a reputation for no nonsense in his court. Due to the nature of the event, they knew they would need a large pool of potential jurors to pick from and more than a 1,000 notices were mailed. The pool to work through was so large, the jury selection part of the trial was set up in the old Pension Building downtown. It was a humongous building that was at least 5 stories high and had a huge open area on the ground floor. That morning, we were escorted to the top floor of the building. Down below we could see they had built a replica of the inside of a court room. It looked like Judge Nunzio was sitting on a large platform. Before him, on one side, were long tables for the defendants and a shorter table on the other side for Touhey and Linsky. Behind them were rows and rows of chairs that were filled by the thousand or so people who had been summoned. Soon, the terrorists filed in, each with their own attorney. It was the first time that I had seen them since the siege ended. Looking down, it was clear that, except for Khaalis, each of the terrorists in our building had changed their appearances. Most now had their heads shaved. If they didn't have a beard, they now bore one. Those who had beards had clean shaven faces. I guess they thought we'd have difficulty identifying them. That was a wrong assumption on their part.

As I stood there I felt a presence and as I glanced to my left, Marion Barry was standing next to me—we were looking down on the scene below. I asked him how he was feeling after he had been shot and he asked me where I was during the terrorist siege. We spoke for a few minutes and returned to our own thoughts as we gazed over the railing.

Soon, we would be called one by one to go down the elevator and walk in front of Nunzio's bench. A court official would then give our names and we would then have to walk from the front of the crowd to the back of the room and back again. The potential jurors were then asked if anyone of them knew us. When I came down, as I stood in front of Nunzio, the terrorists were seated about 15 feet away. I had determined while looking at the scene from above that I was not going to let the terrorist's intimidate me. I looked in their direction and had eye contact with Abdul Latif for a few moments. I was hoping they would get a feeling that I was eager to help put them in jail.

After my name was called, I walked down the long aisle and to my right I noticed a group of women who obviously were family members of the terrorists. Each one had a pad on their laps and as you walked by they took to writing. I knew they wanted me to see they were writing my name.

192

Admittedly, while I was involved in the siege, the terrorists did not want to know my name or anything about me, particularly if they had to kill me. Now, there was an uneasiness arising that they knew my name. Being at the office was one thing, trying to find out where I lived and having Jane and Emily there was quite another. I was already trying to think about things I should do to try and protect my family. It was an unsettling moment.

The trial had started and a number of colleagues had been called to testify. I would see the paper the next day and the local news was filled with coverage. I saw artist renderings of the courtroom and my colleagues. I didn't fully comprehend the same would happen to me shortly. I was finally called to testify towards the middle of the trial. That same day, Jerry Rudman, Marilyn Bargteil and Charles Fenyevesi were called as well. We were told that we'd have police protection and that our families would be able to sit in the courtroom. Jane and Paula came along. We picked up Marilyn in the morning and she would be with us the entire time. Jerry, Marilyn, Charlie and I were led to a room off to the side where a SWAT team was assembled along with a number of armed detectives.

Jerry went first and I was amazed when he was back in the room so quickly. Since his glasses had fallen off at times, they determined that he didn't have much to testify about.

Marilyn and Charlie went next and I was left alone with the police. I was sitting quietly trying to collect my thoughts when a gentleman sat across from me. He introduced himself as the person who was in charge of the District Building during the siege. He spoke very quietly and told me that early on Thursday evening of the siege they brought him and the captain in charge of the mosque situation over to the B'nai B'rith Building to evaluate the rescue plans that might be implemented. He told me they could have rescued the hostages at the other two buildings within a few minutes without negative consequences. They walked the perimeter of the B'nai B'rith Building, had gone in and went up a few floors to look at the obstacles that had been placed in the stairwells and then took a helicopter ride around the building as well.

He then asked me if I knew what he did later that evening. I told him no, but it was evident he was going to tell me. He stopped at his church to pray for our lives. His eyes started to water and he composed himself.

He said the only way we would have come out of that building alive was for a miracle to happen and he was hoping God was hearing his prayers. There was no other way. The rescue attempt would have resulted in numerous deaths. He was glad that we were alive and he felt his prayers had been answered. I held his gaze for a long time as we looked at each other across the table. I was trying to keep my emotions in check and was having difficulty doing so. I thanked him and we shook hands. I never saw that police captain again but will always remember what he looked like and the conversation we had.

Finally they called me. The experience, in terms of intensity of colors and sounds, was eeerily similar to the actual event. Once again, my senses were heightened beyond what I thought possible. It was as if I was having an out of body experience and witnessing what was unfolding from a front row seat rather than being a participant. I was sworn in and seated next to Judge Nunzio. Mark Touhey started handling my questioning and at first wanted me to identify the terrorists in our building. We were advised to identify them by appearance not by names. They didn't want to chance our mixing up any of their Islamic names. I identified the seven terrorists in our building.

Then it started. Touhey and Linsky said they would ask specific questions and didn't want me to tell my "story." I thought, that's easy, I'll just follow their lead. Here was my first question. "Can you tell the court what happened on March 9th on or about 11:00 am?"

Jane said the look on my face was—are you kidding? I began to tell my story and Nunzio exploded. He started yelling at Touhey and Linsky. He had admonished them before—witnesses were not to just tell a story but to answer specific questions.

It was the middle of the trial, a foundation had already been laid. Nunzio appeared to be in a bad mood. They started to take me through my statement via specific questions.

I should have anticipated what was coming later by what had occurred when I gave my original statement. I had identified who had hit me but after thinking about it, I realized it was not that individual but Abdul Adam. This was based on the glasses he was wearing.

I called their office to correct my statement and they said no problem. Unfortunately it was never corrected and we had to go through a whole line of questioning from various defense attorneys and Linsky redirecting to prove it was Adam.

To my chagrin, it was close to lunch and Nunzio took a break; I was instructed to come back after the break. It was not a very enjoyable lunch. Jane, Jerry, Paula and Marilyn were trying to keep my mind off my return engagement.

I was back in the holding room and then brought in to resume where we left off. The various defense attorneys took their turns if they had questions and then Linsky told Nunzio he had a few questions to follow-up. I should have known what was coming by Touhey's body language. He was looking down at the table and doodling on a legal pad and wasn't making eye contact with me.

Linsky walked around the table, stood near me and asked the following question:—"Can you tell the Court what you heard on March 9th on or about 2:00 pm?" Once again, Jane saw my look of astonishment. At first, I wasn't sure if I heard Linsky correctly. I thought about asking him to restate it. However I knew exactly the question he asked and couldn't believe it. My response was: "At about 2:00 pm on Wednesday, March 9th Abdul Adam was listening to a radio and I heard that other buildings were involved in what was happening in Washington, DC. A short time later, Mr Khaalis came into the room where we were being held and announced that his men had succeeded in their endeavor."

Within nano seconds of my declaration, all 12 defense attorneys jumped to their feet and started yelling their objections. They were all talking at once and it was as if mayhem had broken out in the court room. The question and answer drove to the heart of the conspiracy murder charge which carried more onerous consequences for each of the defendants. The defense attorneys were screaming. Touhey and Linsky were sitting, watching it evolve, while Nunzio tried to restore order. Once he did, there was a huge disagreement about what I said and what it actually meant. Did I say endeavor or endeavors and that's what the defense attorneys focused on. What was the definition of each word? Nunzio asked the court reporter to find my exact words. She was having difficulty locating them and that added to the atmosphere.

Nunzio finally turned to me and asked me what I said. I told him I thought I said endeavor and added I was the product of a poor education in

Miami and endeavor to me meant plural. The cascading objections started all over again. I was relieved when Nunzio finally excused me from the stand.

While the trial continued with other testimony, the Green and Rudman families headed to Ocean City for vacation. Jerry and I would sit on the beach each day and try to focus on things other than the siege trial. Though we tried, we couldn't get away from it as we read the *Washington Post* each morning and dealt with our own thoughts. In spite of this, we had a wonderful time. While we were at the beach the trial went to the jury. While we all sat on the beach looking at the waves and watching Emily play in the sand, the jury came back. All the terrorists were found guilty of numerous offenses including kidnapping and armed assault as well as other charges. The two terrorists at the District Building where Maurice Williams was killed were also convicted of murder. The other defendants were acquitted of the felony murder charge. To this day, I believe that all of the terrorists should have shared in the responsibility.

The terrorists at the B'nai B'rith Building and the mosque received sentences of 36 -108 years. The terrorists at the District Building for the killing of Maurice Williams were given life sentences.

The terrorists were assigned to various prisons. Numerous appeals were made on their behalf by defense attorneys. The youngest terrorist was Abdul Hamid, aka Hilvan Finch. Shortly into his sentence, he wrote to Judge Nunzio that he had been a young man when he met Khaalis and had been unduly influenced and was sorry for what he did. Judge Nunzio agreed with Hamid's assessment and arranged for his parole as his appeal was being heard. The prosecution worked to get his sentence reinstated and this dance of Hamid being released and placed back into prison went on for years. His appeal for parole lasted from 1977 until 1987 when the DC Court of Appeals finally upheld Nunzio's original decision. The attorney who worked on the final stages of the appeal which gained his release was Greta Van Susteren—one of the unbelievable ironies that I uncovered. An irony not only because of her status as a known celebrity on Fox News, but because I personally know Greta and had occasionally worked and interacted with her from 2002 through 2009. Jonathan Kempner hired me at the Mortgage Bankers Association when he was the group's President. I soon learned that his sister-in-law was Greta Van Susteren. We had her moderate general sessions at a number of our annual meetings. In all the time that we worked together I did not know about her efforts to have a terrorist released who had held me hostage. Though Jonathan was intimately familiar with the history of the event, I don't believe that Greta knew of my history and connection. Once again, I'm not sure I have a calculator that can compute the odds of this circumstance.

CHAPTER THIRTY EIGHT

NEVER FORGOTTEN

Thirty-four years after the event, the world has changed in many ways and has also remained the same. Unfortunately for many, the notion and theme that Khaalis spoke to us about, that Jews have created the ills of the world, have not abated. Through ignorance and lack of understanding new generations are exposed to the anti-Semitic vitriol Khaalis used as an excuse to attack the B'nai B'rith building. Beyond the District Building and the mosque which also had specific reasons of choice, the B'nai B'rith Building was chosen because it was a Jewish institution just as the terrorists in Munich attacked the Israeli delegation at the Olympics. The fuse that Khaalis lit 34 years ago still simmers every day. It's a sad commentary on human nature.

We were extremely fortunate no one died in our building. Though I never met him, I still think of Maurice Williams and the tragic early termination of his life. I know that his family and friends still mourn the loss of a life that held such promise.

I watched Marion Barry's career with both his successes and human frailties that he continues to exhibit. We never met again, yet I feel a connection from that short conversation we had 34 years ago.

Over the 34 years after the event, I lost contact with many of my former colleagues. As I stared the project of writing about the siege, I reconnected with a number of them to gain their perspectives and listen to their stories. As we met, it was as if we never lost contact. The 40 hours we experienced together created a unique bond that has never been broken.

One prime example occurred in the spring of 2009. Jane and I and my brothers and sisters-in-laws Bob and Alice Ramer and Steven and Barbara Gurtov traveled to Israel for 16 days. I had visited Israel on business in 1975 and 1978 and I was looking forward to seeing the changes in the country. The tour company Steven selected was based in South Florida and there were three bus loads of participants.

On the second day of the tour, we were visiting a kibbutz with a shoe factory and had stopped for people to make purchases. I was speaking with Wendy, the tour company owner, and exchanging stories on where we each lived and she mentioned living in Washington, many years ago.

She asked what brought me to Washington and I told her B'nai B'rith. She said "That's funny-one of her tour guides on the blue bus had worked for B'nai B'rith and had been involved in a hostage incident." Dumbfounded I asked her his name and she said David Leshnick. I asked her where David was at that moment and she said inside the shoe factory. I found Jane and told her to come with me for she was not going to believe what was about to happen.

When I worked with David he had long black hair and a black beard. I found him in the back of the store with a clean shaven head and no beard. He still looked like the David I knew though a Mr. Clean version. I walked up to him and said—David Leshnick–and as he turned to look at me he stopped. He recognized me immediately and we hugged. I introduced Jane and he hugged her as well. We had not seen one another in 33 years and it was as if it was yesterday that he was shaking his head no and I was nodding yes. For the next 14 days we had a chance to catch up. When we were in Jerusalem for that part of the tour, Jane and I went to David's apartment where we met his wife Dorit and two of his children. It was an added dimension to our trip that I never dreamed of.

As I looked for colleagues to see where they might be, I ran across articles on the Internet about their work and lives. In a number of instances I found personal references to their experience as hostages. My former colleague Lew Hamburger was profiled on storyofmylife.com in 2009. Lew stated, "It's all about trust and realizing how simple life really is" Lew, who is often asked about his own story when trust in a terrorist's ability not to fire his weapon was the only thing between Lew and sudden death—a moment which infused in Lew the ability to look at the way he handled life in a whole new light. More than 100 of my colleagues during the 40 hours were having personal discussions with themselves on the meaning of their lives up to that point. Would there be additional chapters? Lew was wondering if he'd be at his daughter's Bat Mitzvah the following Saturday?

As I reached out to a number of colleagues after all these years, I wasn't sure what the reaction would be. Some were happy to hear from me and others never returned my notes or calls. I fully understand and respect any reluctance they might feel. I was saddened when I researched where colleagues might be and found they had passed away. For those I was able to speak with, I am forever grateful. I had a chance to catch up on the joys and challenges in their lives.

Lawrie Kaplan, now in his late 70's, has worked with his wife Candi in the very successful insurance business that she built. His son Jonathan, who chided me at O'Hare for littering when he was just a child, speaks a number of languages and is a respected academic who lives in various parts of the world. Lawrie and Candi had a daughter who works in the insurance business as well. Lawrie is also a cancer survivor and still maintains that Chicago toughness he always exhibited.

Marilyn Bargteil's first marriage ended and she remarried. They live in the Maryland suburbs. She still works for B'nai B'rith on a part time basis. Her two young daughters, Dee and Michelle have grown into accomplished women. Dee lives in Israel with her family and Michelle in Rhode Island. Marilyn and Robert have faced a number of health issues, yet her resilience is incredible to watch. For me, I don't have to wonder where Marilyn draws upon the internal fortitude to face what life has to offer. 34 years ago, a life lessen gave her that reservoir of resources to call upon.

I found BJ Neal, at the time 80 years old, also living in the Maryland suburbs with the boyfriend she married, Ira. I arranged to take BJ out to coffee where we spent five hours catching up and discussing the terrorist siege and the important role she played. When I picked her up, Ira, now 85, checked me out to make sure his wife would be ok with this guy. He looked me over and said—I remember you—drive carefully and he gave BJ a kiss. I promised to bring her back safely. The five hours we spent together is something I'll remember the rest of my life. In early January, I received a note from Marilyn asking if I'd be going to BJ's memorial and that's how I found out that BJ had become ill in the fall and within a short time had passed away. She would have been 81 a week or so after she died. I went to her memorial in the lobby of her apartment complex. I was able to offer Ira and BJ's children and other relatives my condolences and see a number of colleagues that I had not spoken with in 34 years. Though sad at the occasion, I smiled within my mind when I thought of BJ and the conversation we had in July 2010. She was still that pretty, straight talking and sassy lady I knew 34 years prior. I also knew that my timing for writing the book was apropos. How lucky I was to have captured BJ's story. Her courage in the face of adversity I will always admire. I know fully that her actions during those 40 hours contributed to our ability to walk out alive. Thank you BJ and I hope I told your part of the story as you would have wanted me to.

CHAPTER THIRTY NINE

ARDESHIR AND ME

In my work we engage a widely respected event photographer, Abbas Shirmohammadi, who I knew was born in Iran and had immigrated to the United States and built a successful business. One day I told Abbas of my writing and I wondered—did he actually know Ambassador Zahedi? Though he met him only once and conveyed the story to me, he did have a friend Nasser Ovissi a well known painter from Iran who was personal friends with the ambassador. Soon, I found myself speaking with Ovissi by phone explaining who I was, asking if he would make the initial contact which he graciously agreed to do. A short time later, I was given a fax number so that I could provide a letter of introduction. When I sent my letter to the ambassador, I told him that he and I were extrinsically linked 33 years ago. We just didn't know it. I also thanked him for his efforts that allowed me to enjoy a productive and happy life with my wife Jane and our now two grown daughters Emily and Jessica, my son-in-law Bryan and the grandchildren—Gillian, Harry and Thomas who have followed. I explained I was writing the book and would he agree to an interview. Literally a day later I received a message on my office phone and cell phone from the Ambassador. He was astounded to have heard from an individual involved in the siege after 33 years. He told me in the message that he remembered every detail. When we first spoke he said he'd be pleased to do the interview but he lives in Switzerland. My response was as soon as he could find a convenient time frame I would come to meet him. That night I asked Jane how she would like a one day trip to Switzerland and she said, Switzerland would be wonderful, but we'll be going for at least 10 days. When my brother and sister-in-law Bobby and Alice Ramer found out about the developing adventure, they said they were in and would be traveling with us.

As the ambassador and I worked on the details for the visit, we exchanged numerous faxes and had a number of warm phone conversations. We were finally able to coordinate schedules and in July 2010, we traveled to Montreux for the interview. With much anticipation, he arranged to pick me up at the Montreux Palace where we were staying. I told him I'd take a cab but he insisted on coming for me. The plan was for the ambassador and I to spend the afternoon together at his villa and then later that evening Jane, Bobby, Alice and I would go back to the villa for dinner. As I waited for the 2:00 pm pickup, I told Jane and Bobby and Alice to come out side and wait with me. At the appointed hour, a black Mercedes sedan pulled up and out popped Ardeshir Zahedi. He was wearing slacks, a shirt that was not tucked in and sandals. He was also wearing racing gloves for driving. He walked around the car to me and we shook hands for a long time as he put his other hand on my shoulder. I then introduced him to my family. Jane and Alice were immediately taken in by the old world charm as he kissed their hands and he greeted Bobby.

When we were alone in the car, the bonding we started to feel was almost instantaneous. It was as if two old friends who had not seen one another for 33 years were starting to catch up on what life had brought to each of our door steps. He gave me a brief history of the villa and his life in Montreux. The villa had originally been purchased by his father who was also a historic figure in Iranian history. As I entered and looked at the surroundings and the array of historical pictures and memorabilia, I found it hard to comprehend the opportunity that had been afforded me. For a history major in undergraduate school, this was like a dream come true. For more than 40 years, the ambassador had personal relationships with what seemed like every world leader and he had the pictures, notes and gifts to prove it.

As we began our discussions about the siege, he quickly proved that even at 82, his mind and memory remained sharp and clear. I thought I was going to need to ask questions to prod memories. That was far from the case. We agreed that he would talk and I would interject questions for clarification or provide insight from the inside. For almost five hours we shared our first hand recollections and were able to reach further understanding of situations and circumstances that were developing over the 40 hours. From firsthand knowledge I knew how bad it truly was and the ambassador confirmed it for me. He shared with me the fears, and at times helpless thoughts, he had about trying to end the terrorist siege peacefully. He told me the stories he conveyed to Khaalis from his background and diplomatic experience to try and find some opening to have Khaalis reach an understanding that it was better to release his hostages. As he looked at me, he further shared the story that he utilized that finally created the moment where Khaalis began to look for a way to end the siege without further harm to me and my colleagues. It was a highly emotional and informative five hours. When I asked the ambassador where this event fit into his extensive diplomatic career, he told me it was one of the most important negotiations he had ever conducted and intense periods in his life. He relayed the story of how he felt seeing his father for the first time following his father's release from prison after a number of years and how shocked he was. Upon being summoned back to Washington to participate in the negotiations, he had similar feelings in viewing the city under siege. He knew he had to be successful to try and save lives and failure was not an option. As we finished the initial interview session, I also knew that no one had ever captured the full details of the ambassador's story and his critical role and I felt privileged that he shared it with me.

That evening we had an incredibly delightful dinner with the ambassador and the president of our hotel and his wife. We spoke further about the siege as well as world and current Iranian affairs. We were treated as old family members. We were exposed to his wonderful sense of humor, down to earth view of life and his love of stuffed animals that played music and adorned his father's original dining room table. We laughed a lot at dinner and took photos of each other. The next night he insisted that we join him at one of his favorite restaurants at the Fairmont Hotel overlooking Lake Geneva. The staff set up his usual table including the pillow for his chair to help relieve stress on his bad back. It was like being in the presence of a rock star as he was greeted by people throughout the evening. Our discussions continued. Jane commented afterward that it was like she and Bobby and Alice were not there, for he truly wanted to concentrate on me and how we were attached more than three decades ago in an event that had an impact on both our lives.

As the evening wound down, I said to the Ambassador that in my wildest dreams, I never thought that I would have a personal relationship with the former Ambassador to the United States from Iran, the Shah's former son-in-law and a world renowned diplomat. He looked at me and said he had similar feelings that he would have a relationship with me. I certainly didn't take offense and fully understood his meaning. He said he and I were like old friends who have shared a common bond that no one could ever take away. When we walked him to his car after dinner, he kissed Jane and Alice's hands, warmly shook Bobby's hand and he came over to me and hugged me. He held on to me for a number of minutes. It was almost as a father would hug a son. He told me to be well and to stay in touch.

After we returned home he left a message for me to call him to let him know that we had arrived safely. During our trip around Switzerland after our meeting in Montreux, we found a stuffed animal that played cymbals that we thought he would like to add to his collection. We sent it along with another memento. Among his memorabilia, he had a signed football from former Washington Redskins Coach George Allen in a glass case. As a young man, the Ambassador traveled around America quite extensively and received his undergraduate degree from Utah State University where he enjoyed football and other sports. I had a signed football from Steve Young and I sent it on to the ambassador noting though it wasn't from a Utah State player, Steve Young had a strong Utah connection. The ambassador remembered his Utah State team lost to Brigham Young quite badly in 1949. I suspect Steve's ball is proudly displayed next to George's.

Ardeshir Zahedi and I were linked in a unique historical event that we continue to think about on a regular basis. The worlds where we lived our lives were not even in the same galactic orbit. However, the ability of man to be inhumane to his fellow man and impact lives that had no relation to the grievances that provoked these actions created a friendship that took 34 years to nurture. Ambassador Zahedi's work and the dedicated efforts of many others that I met and have written about helped save our lives. I will always be indebted to my friend's selfless actions and his desire to save people's lives.

CHAPTER FORTY

PATRICK MULLANY

Doing my research, I came across a name that I had not seen before– Patrick Mullany–an FBI official. After further investigation I learned that he was one of four experts on terrorism and hostage negotiation the FBI employed. For those of us who live in this wonderful time of the Internet, researching and finding people has become scarily easy. I thought, maybe he was a fairly young man in the 1970's and was still around. That he is. I found that Patrick had retired from the FBI in the early 1980's, had done other security work, some on an international basis, and had finally settled in Indian Wells, California. He became a council member and in November 2010, had been elected Mayor. I sent Patrick an introductory email and like the ambassador, he left me a voice mail message that evening. He was astounded to have heard from a victim from what he described as probably the most important case he handled in his career. In January 2011, he and I met for lunch and spent hours discussing what the police, FBI, State Department, White House and other agencies were doing to keep us alive. He also told me in vivid detail how he had sat next to the ambassadors during the long grueling hours of negotiation with Khaalis. He confirmed for me everything the ambassador described. We filled each other in on what was happening from our side of the siege. We both knew how bad it was and as we covered various aspects that were occurring at particular times, we would both grow quiet. We were thinking about how close the situation came to going bad and we were involved in a circumstance that was on a razors edge. At times, as we spoke one of us would feel our eyes welling up as the feelings and emotions from almost 34 years ago became just as raw and real as they did when the event was unfolding. What truly stood out in Patrick's mind after the siege had ended was that it did so because of the incredible cooperation among a multiple of agencies and organizations, both domestic and international. In 1977, he felt that was a highly unusual occurrence and it was a major factor in saving us.

On behalf of all of my colleagues, I was able to thank Patrick for his efforts in saving our lives.

CHAPTER FORTY ONE

THE TERRORISTS

After the trial concluded, the terrorists were convicted of numerous offenses. On September 6, 1977, Judge Nunzio sentenced all those involved. The terrorists involved at the B'nai B'rith Building received the following sentences:

Hamas Abdul Khaalis was sentenced to 41 to 123 years. He remained in prison until November 13, 2003. On that day, Khaalis died at the Federal Complex Prison in Butler, North Carolina. He was 81 years old.

Abdul Latif, aka Carl E. Roper, was sentenced from 36 to 108 years. He was released from prison in 1991. He's in his late 60's.

Abdul Shaheed, aka Marvin Sadler, was sentenced from 36 to 108 years. He will not be released from prison until 2048. He's in his late 50's.

Abdul Salaam, aka Clarence White, received a 40 to 120 year sentence. He died in prison in 2001 at the age of 55.

Abdul Hamid, aka Hilvan Jude Finch, was sentenced from 36 to 108 years and was released from prison in 1981 and his parole upheld in 1987.

Abdul Adam, aka George W. Smith, was sentenced from 44 to 132 years. The man who hit me in the face with the rifle, slashed Wes Hymes with a machette and almost killed Alton Kirkland. He petitioned the court in May 2001 to seek parole using the same reasoning that Abdul Hamid successfully deployed to gain his release. At that time, the court rejected his argument. He was finally released from prison in June, 2010. He is in his mid-60s. James Sweeney, an Assistant United States Attorney who defended the parole request on behalf of the government was assigned the case in the early 2000s. In a conversation he indicated to me that working on the case had a profound impact on him and he thought about the siege on a regular basis.

Abdul Hazzaaq, aka Nelson McQueen Jr., was sentenced from 40 to 120 years. He will not be released from prison until 2055. He's in his late 50s.

CHAPTER FORTY TWO

A PERSONAL POSTSCRIPT

Jane never did finish that physical therapy degree. The siege impacted her in a way that motivated her to look at a career where she could be self-supporting. As other relatives during the siege, she thought about how she would support herself and Emily if I did not survive. She never wanted to be in that position of uncertainty again. Through a lot of hard work and effort she took the prerequisite accounting classes that allowed her to obtain her CPA. Today, she's the chief financial officer of a large cardiac practice.

Emily, two years old at the time, grew up. We discovered a beautiful voice as she prepared for her Bat Mitzvah and a knack for acting which she utilized in high school and college. Today, she's a grown woman, living with her husband Bryan and her children Gillian, Harry and Thomas. Jane and I talk about them as our grandchildren rather than Emily and Bryan's kids. She's a successful entrepreneur having started a private school in the Seattle area where they live.

Our daughter Jessica was born three years after the terrorist siege. There were moments from March 9 – 11, 1977, where perhaps Emily would not have had a sibling with me as the father. Jess is the true artist in our family. Her painting and photography led to a fine arts degree in undergraduate school and a year of study in Venice, Italy produced the masters in computer graphic design. Always looking for something more to experience in life, she's about to embark on obtaining a nursing degree to compliment her compassion for people. Jess and partner Meridyth live near us.

As I finished this book, Jane and I were in New York City. We went to the World Trade Center site to pay our respects. As I walked near Ground Zero and visited St. Paul's Chapel I worked hard to control my emotions. I believe I came out of the terrorist siege at B'nai B'rith fairly well intact emotionally. However, at some rare times, like visiting Ground Zero, there are deeply placed emotions which bubble up. Surely what happened to us pales in comparison to what transpired on 9/11, just as the Holocaust and its enormity has no comparison to other historical events. Then, just two days later, Navy Seals carry out the successful raid on Osama Bin Laden's compound and he is killed. To be in New York, to visit the site and then to have Bin Laden tracked down and killed while there provided the fuel for a multitude of emotions and thoughts to erupt. Was this a further coincidence or another irony on this journey in telling the story of the first major terrorism event?

In many respects, I believe the event my colleagues and I lived made me a better person. I tried not to take myself so seriously and to take advantage of all that life has to offer. As others who have experienced stressful circumstances that potentially could end their lives, you have choices on how to handle the stress and emotions that remain. I feel sorry for people who need crutches such as alcohol or drugs or dangerous behavior to cope, though I have some understanding of their looking to find a way to deal with remnants of pain from such events. I know I was lucky. For some reason I had some internal fortitude to put the siege into perspective and harness the experience in a positive way.

Robert Liss, the *Miami Herald* reporter who interviewed me soon after the terrorist siege (I found out later he was dying of cancer and writing a book on his own life threatening experience) asked me what was different in my life from just a few days event. I told him the color of the blue sky, which I always enjoyed, was more intense and clear then it had ever been. Thirty-four years later, the color of that blue sky is still as intense and incredible to behold.

My Thanks
Over the last year and a half, I received encouragement, help and guidance from numerous people. This project could not have been completed without their support:

My former colleague and dear friend Jim Fowler edited the entire manuscript and helped make this story coherent. His counsel and suggestions were immeasurable in getting the project to this point. In life, one gets to make various choices. One of them is choosing your friends and in Jim I know I had done so wisely. Any mistakes one might find are mine.

My niece Sara Garick always provided positive feedback whether deserved or not. She became one of my early readers and her encouragement helped me to keep focused on completing the book. She kept her husband Bob up at night doing so.

My sister and brother-in-law Alice and Bob Ramer became traveling companions for trips related to the book project. They were always excited about the interviews I conducted and offered positive feelings about work being completed. Alice never failed to mention the book to people she knew and was constantly looking for publishers and agents on my behalf.

My brother and sister-in-law Steven and Barbara Gurtov offered encouragement and patience as I would cover the events to be included in the book.

A thank you to my niece Amy Meadows, a professional writer and editor with her own company, Green Meadows Communications LLC in Atlanta, Georgia. Her suggestions on the book's structure and feedback were very helpful.

Numerous friends, colleagues and acquaintances offered support and advice and read chapters. My thanks particularly to Leah Logan, Elaine Howard, Ann Gambaro, Adina Holmes, Dan Thoms, Jerry Aust, Chaya Zahn, Patti McGraw, Debbie McGeady, Suzanne Hurley, Kimberly Newell, Venita Murray, Phyllis Roberts, Julie Dychkewich, Masuda Ranjber ,Norm Edwards, Deanna Johnston, Shirlene Datcher, Geri Carlisle, Bennie Murphy, Diego Prudencio, Patti Miller, Mark Brady, Debbie Santasania, Andy Stack, Mike Wheeden, Faith Cooper, Andi Miller, Shelley Reback, Steve O'Connor, Sandra Troutman, Vicki Vidal, Phyllis Slesinger, Cheryl Crispen, Sarah Tinsley Demarest, John Courson, David Kittle, John Robbins, Michael Murray, Michael Sorohan, Janet Hewitt, Anne Marie Munson, Sam Reed, executives from the mortgage banking industry who participated in the Future Leaders program and were forced to listen to my stories.

Dear friends Allan and Karen Mann who were updated on the adventure every Friday night during date night, Dennis Friedman the managing partner of the cardiac practice where Jane is CFO and his wife Sandra always took an interest and gave positive feedback and my next door neighbor Jim Tierney, a Justice Department attorney who would politely listen and give advice as we stood in the middle of the street in all kinds of weather.

A special acknowledgement to Sharon Bryce, who along with Jane helps make the cardiac practice they manage successful. As a family friend, she has offered positive comments and feedback. Her unfailing belief that I would succeed was sincerely appreciated. She has dibs on playing BJ in the movie, so I need to get that done as well.

My daughter Emily and son-in-law Bryan always gave support and encouragement as the book unfolded. To my grandchildren Gillian, Harry and Thomas. It is my sincerest hope when they are old enough to read it, they'll view it as a legacy and learn from it.

To my daughter Jessica who put aside her bias that I was her father and offered an honest assessment from reading and re-reading the manuscript. She provided insight on how the 30-something population might relate to the book. Her enthusiasm and commitment for the project was a source of inspiration.

Finally, to my wife Jane. I've always told people the best thing that ever happened to me almost 40 years ago was when she agreed to be my partner, friend and love of life. Any success I've enjoyed has been achieved in large measure because of her support, encouragement and strong belief that I could obtain goals that I set. She offered perspective, thoughts and direction for the book over the year and a half of researching and writing. She never doubted that I would complete this project. We've been graced with good health, a wonderful family and opportunities that have made our life fun. The two of us have always appreciated that fact.

Forgotten Hostages Website

It was recognized the book needed to be of a finite length to try and create an enjoyable reading journey for those experiencing the event. There were additional details about people mentioned and related stories that while interesting, included might have interrupted the flow of the book.

As I finished up the book and discussed these additions with my editing team, I decided the best way to bring these to readers was through a website dedicated to the book.

So, www.ForgottenHostages.com was developed. It is my hope this website will establish *Forgotten Hostages* more as a living book where thoughts, comments and new details, even over more than 30 years later can be added and not forgotten.

Made in the USA
Columbia, SC
14 May 2021

37252022R00124